Donated by

St. Marys Box Co.

In Memory of

Blain Earl Kitchen

GUIDE TO
Pheasant Hunting

GUIDE TO
Pheasant Hunting

M. D. JOHNSON

PHOTOGRAPHY BY JULIA C. JOHNSON

STACKPOLE
BOOKS

Published by
STACKPOLE BOOKS
5067 Ritter Road
Mechanicsburg, PA 17055
www.stackpolebooks.com

Printed in China

First edition

10 9 8 7 6 5 4 3 2 1

Photographs by Julia C. Johnson, except where otherwise noted

Library of Congress Cataloging-in-Publication Data

Johnson, M. D.
    Guide to pheasant hunting / M.D. Johnson ; photography by
Julia C. Johnson.— 1st ed.
        p.   cm.
    Includes index.
    ISBN-13: 978-0-8117-0176-1
    ISBN-10: 0-8117-0176-X
    1. Pheasant shooting.   I. Title.

SK325.P5J64 2006
799.2'4625—dc22
                                    2005027483

Contents

*To my mother—Carolyn Sue Johnson—who endured
years upon years of predawn wakeups, muddy steps, hairy dogs,
feathers in the basement, and dead things in the fridge.*

*Thanks so much for listening and for always—
always—being right there. I love you, Ma.*

Acknowledgments

A LOT OF TIME WENT INTO THIS BOOK. TIME measured not in weeks or months, but in years. In generations. And in lifetimes.

There are a lot of miles here, too, and places that read like a geography lesson. Oregon's Willamette Valley. Hershey, Pennsylvania. Pierre, South Dakota. Williamsburg, Iowa. Mount Sterling, Ohio . . . and the list goes on and on and on like the distance between the towns in the Nebraska Sandhills.

And people. Lots of people. Faces, names, pictures. Richard Creason and his grandmother's Savage .410 single-shot in South Dakota. A bearded Bruce Meredith in Tygh Valley, Oregon. John Taranto's first rooster . . . and my Grandpa Verity's last. They're all here.

My role here, if you're wondering, isn't so much an author as a collector. Within these 140-some odd pages is a collection of—well—memories. No, make that experiences. How this, and why that. A remember when, or two. Oh, there are things to be learned, certainly, but more so, there are things to be felt. And to be shared over and over and over again. But I digress. . . .

This collection of pheasants and pheasant hunting belongs to a great many people, people whom I have had the pleasure, the honor, and the privilege of spending time with over . . . well, the truth is, I'm not sure how long it's been. Damn near thirty-five years, if I'm doing the math right. And in those three-plus decades, I've crossed paths with some of the most extraordinary people on the planet. This, then, is their book, for it reveals their experiences. Their successes and their failures. Their laughter and their tears. These are folks who truly know—and appreciate— the beauty that is the frost on the goldenrod and the Queen Anne's lace. These are people who live for tattered canvas britches, the rich aroma of pipe tobacco, and a trio of black dogs rattlin' through a stand of switchgrass. They've been privy to many a skulking cockbird as he weaves his streamlined way through the wild rose and the bromegrass, and they've come to enjoy—nah, need—his cackled curses. They know who they are. They don't have to tell you "I'm a pheasant hunter." And neither—about them, that is—do I.

And so, to all of you, a very sincere and heartfelt *thank you*, for you have contributed much more than simply words or theories, strategies or techniques in a book. You've given to me and mine of yourselves, and you've helped me grow as a man, an individual, and a hunter. Some day I'll find a way to repay you all, but until then:

To Tony "Jakeman" Miller—Thanks, brother, for keeping me on track, for serving as a first-rate sounding board, and for listening through each and every one of my "I hate this job" tirades.

To Phil Bourjaily—For your patience, expertise, and friendship, I am forever grateful. I can't choose the *best* time we've shared afield, because it's all been excellent. And with this, your wait is over.

To Lee "Spoonie" Harstad—Thanks for all the incredible outdoor opportunities you've provided us over the years. Couldn't have done it without you and Maggie. *South Dakota rocks!!*

what? . . . thirty-three years since the Daisy BB-gun and my "first" fox squirrel in Dzedo's Woods. I only hope I can grow to be half the teacher and mentor you are. Love you.

To Dave Fountain—I'm not sure you realize to what extent, but your friendship has made our transition from Washington to Iowa much, much easier. Thanks for the open-door policy . . . and give that bad dog a whoop'n, will ya!?

To Maggie, Jet, and Deacon—Three of the finest black Lab dogs—and best friends—a body could ever hope for. I'm honored to have been there for the first rooster, and I'll weep when I'm there for the last. Thanks for all your hard work.

To Shadow, Ike, Molly, Ebonee, and all the others I've had the pleasure of spending time with afield— Your contribution to each and every hunt was 150 percent, and all you asked was a soft pat, a hug around the neck, and a piece of Little Debbie oatmeal pie. Your performances were stellar.

To Sam Gaston, Chuck Hillas, Jimmy Carlson, Jerry Davis, Ken Kemper, Duke and Kay Dusheck, Jim Schmitz, Gary Smith, Richard and Diana Kieffer, Mike Purtz, Steve Smith, Howard Klingeman, Dale and Doris Newman, and the dozens upon dozens of folks across the country who have welcomed me and mine into your homes and onto your ground—this is *your* book, for without your hospitality, I never would have experienced the outdoors in the ways I have been so fortunate to have seen it. A mere *thank you* seems insignificant, but . . . *thank you.*

And, finally, to Julia Carol Johnson, my award-winning outdoor photographer, my best friend, my wife, and my partner. You've survived—what?—five of these projects now with me? Your application for sainthood is en route to heaven, even as we speak! Your work is outstanding, and your patience without equal. I love you, Julia . . . I really do.

To Bruce Knodel—I said it before, sir, and I'll say it again. Thank you so much for volunteering your time to present my father and me with our hunter education course back in March of '72. No idea what you were starting, eh?

To my father, Mick—Wow, Pop! I really don't know where to begin. It's been an unbelievable . . .

Foreword

THEY HAUNT YOU, THESE COCKBIRDS. Attentive and catlike, my English setter Radar keeps his bright eyes and wet nose locked on a skulking ringneck that just won't play fair. It moves through cover nasty enough to draw blood. My tricolored bird dog adjusts, body trembling, plumed tail erect. The pheasant darts off through nearby swampy cover like a copper-colored snake with a long streaming tail, and my canine partner hungrily follows.

This upland bird, he won't go easily.

As if it isn't tough enough to get pheasants into the air and within shotgun range, the flush itself will unnerve you. The cockbird's cackling clatter is a defiant curse thrown at us wingshooters, yet we admire this bird for his fire and tenacity. That long tail is a distraction as the ringneck rises up, and the bird seems to be such a big target that we end up directing colorful language at ourselves after missing "such an easy shot."

He's a white-collared, clown-faced, wild-eyed, buff-brown, copper-colored, brilliant-bodied, wing-clattering, spur-toting, tail-barred devil of a bird, and we love him and the landscapes where we find him.

Whether we hunt them in wild, dreamlike places or on either-sex shooting preserves where the birds are planted like presents wrapped especially for dog men and shooters, pheasants stand up and demand our attention. We find them in eastern swamps, where cockbirds flush full of those curses the moment we try to work that cover. In midwestern cornfields, they hang in the scrubby cover along farm lots and unexpected places we never imagined.

Pheasants are runners, and where you first find one might not be where you take your shot. From East Coast to West, from South Dakota to Kansas to Nebraska, we can find ringnecks so long as there is off-season nesting habitat for hardy hens and elbow room in season to work a Lab or another pheasant-crazed canine. Elsewhere we might even put on a dogless pheasant drive with stationed blockers—and still they might escape. Such strategies make them fun birds to hunt.

But, oh, they can be underhanded.

SOUTH DAKOTA TOURISM

As a Pennsylvania native, I was first introduced to ringnecks during mixed-bag hunts with my dad's beagle Pokey. On rabbits, she ruled, but upland birds got some attention too—ringnecks definitely included.

Once, in wide-open cover, she paused, tail moving like a windshield wiper. A clump of weeds no bigger than a case of shotshells drew her attention. "Rabbit—get ready," my father whispered, and I waited for that bounding cottontail. *Cak-c-a-ak, cak-cak*, protested the hypothetical bunny, and we watched openmouthed—armed yet off balance—as a brilliant Keystone State cockbird, perfectly legal that season, climbed away and sailed to safety.

Sneaky? Got that right. Still haven't had enough? Well *Guide to Pheasant Hunting* is just the thing for you. . . .

Both serious hunters and outdoor professionals, M. D. and Julie Johnson capture the delight—and yes, despair—of chasing these marvelous gamebirds. Such a well-researched and predictably heartfelt book can provide sustained pleasure in off times when you can't go afield and during those posthunt, woodstove evenings with gun dogs gathered at your side and a brace of hard-won pheasants on the kitchen countertop. Enjoy.

Steve Hickoff
Kittery, Maine
July 2005

Introduction

FOR A WRITER, THERE ARE FEW THINGS AS—well, I guess *intimidating* is as good a word as I have available—as a blank computer screen. It used to be a blank legal pad, but time and technology have changed that . . . for the better, I guess, but I'm not entirely sure. Legal pads, for one, don't power down, a techno-term for hitting the OFF button, unexpectedly and by themselves, thus erasing everything you've done. However, I digress. . . .

A blank screen. That's literally what I'm starting with here. Figuratively, however, my so-called screen is anything but blank. Yeah, those of you who know me, go right on ahead and laugh—"M. D. . . . yeah. A blank screen. Makes sense." Some days, they're close to being right, I'll give 'em that much.

I'm talking about this figurative blank screen, and how that phrase relates to this book on pheasant hunting. More perhaps than did our other books—on hunting ducks, turkeys, small game, geese—this one dredged up memories and touched on experiences that I can only think of as nostalgic. Traditional, maybe, but nostalgic is a good word, too.

I don't know exactly what it is about ring-necked pheasants that takes me back. Back to a hundred-acre family farm on what was then the outskirts of a small town in northeastern Ohio—a farm now paved and home to such rooster-free facilities as Robbie Lee's Banquet Hall, Newton Village Apartments, and St. Mike's Byzantine Catholic Church. The pheasants, I'm afraid, are gone, as is the couple who farmed the ground and raised the six children who grew up there . . . back in those "pheasants were everywhere" days.

Pheasants take me back to a tricolored beagle dog named Nellie, who every year would give birth to perfectly healthy pups in a hole dug under a perfectly good doghouse. "Listen to her bark," the Old Man would say. "Her bark changes when she's on a bird. It's more of a *yip* than a bark." And he was right. I don't know why—canine excitement?—but he was right. Pheasants take me back, too, to a time long before computers were a necessary evil, before those infuriating Internet forums whose followers preach "Use this shotgun" and "Use this shotshell" came into vogue. It was before fashion in the field outweighed functionality, when every canvas coat came with a can of Copenhagen and a rich brown wide-wale collar.

This was a time of Old Men, with their salty language lessons about Life, and of posthunt dimly lit taverns where, quietly behind their sweating cans of cola, young ears learned everything there was to know about cars, women, dogs, shotguns, opening day, and rooster pheasants.

What is it about pheasants that mine these memories, resurrecting things that for many of us were forged so long ago? I can't point a finger at a single element, for there are many. The men—the hunters—and the dogs. The cold and the canvas. A tattered pair of Northerner boots and a Stevens side-by-side, choked full. True, it's Mister Ringneck, as well, a bird that has rolled with a thousand agricultural punches, any one of which might have extirpated a lesser species. And it's not because we haven't tried, what with fenceline-to-fenceline farming, a mad scientist's mix of pesticides and herbicides, and fleets of batch trucks emblazoned with the heart-wrenching logo—*Cover it with Asphalt*. Somehow, some way, by the grace of God, the ring-necked pheasant has survived. "Too ornery, he is," the old-timers who are left will tell you. "Too ornery to die out completely." I'd dearly love to believe the Old Men are right.

But maybe—just maybe—it's more about where pheasants live, more even than the birds themselves. Near a sod house on the Nebraska prairie, a pair—rooster and hen—scratch among the yellowed cotton-wood leaves, not acknowledging or even recognizing a panoramic view we humans could only picture as

forever. From the edge of a cut wheatfield in eastern Washington best described as infinite, a hen, brood in tow, chases grasshoppers through the dusty, fallen remnants of a Pacific Rim volcano. And on a narrow spit of sand stretching out into the current of the South Platte River, a lusty rooster cackles the dawn awake as the Front Range explodes into a painter's palette of color.

It's these visions of places the ringneck calls home that take us back. Back to a time when we followed the Old Man, tentative steps in too big three-buckler boots and a wood-stocked Daisy—we didn't know it didn't work, nor did we care—held at the finest port arms that a seven-year-old could manage. We owe the ringneck a living, this Chinese import turned native. We owe it respect. And occasionally, as we stand on the highest

point during the tenth month of the year and watch as the sun slips behind the maples and the oaks and the pines, we owe it our thanks—thanks for not allowing us to forget those who came before us or those destined to come after.

It's been twenty-nine years since I slipped that first wild rooster into my game bag. Today, almost three decades later, I can still feel the Old Man's hand on my shoulder and his "Good job, Son" smile that spoke volumes without his saying a word. Closing my eyes, I can still feel the jolt from the 16-gauge autoloader and see the smoke as it rolled out of the muzzle to meld with the cold Ohio winter. It was a good thing then, and it's a good thing now. I envy those of you who can close your eyes and relive the same memories.

We hope you enjoy this work. It's meant to educate and it's meant to entertain. But most of all, it's meant to remind you of the people, the places, and the visions that come courtesy of one of our wild treasures—the ring-necked pheasant.

M. D. and Julie Johnson,
along with Maggie, Jet, Deacon,
and a host of characters
September 2005

CHAPTER 1

Meet the Players

I WAS BORN IN OHIO IN 1964 AND, HAVING BEEN born in Ohio in 1964, I never knew a time when there weren't pheasants in the Buckeye State. Sure, there may have been only two or three—statewide, mind you—but there were always pheasants.

My father, Mick, came into the world in March 1940, and he recalls that when he was a young man in the 1950s, there were quite a few pheasants on the old home place. "You'd see 'em most days in your Babi's flower beds, picking, wandering around in the yard," he'd say, gazing off into the distance in hopes of seeing a farm long gone, replaced—unfortunately for the pheasants that once lived there—by a banquet hall and an apartment complex. "It wasn't difficult to go out back or to John Tobin's down the street and find a couple roosters and a rabbit in an afternoon."

Today, though there are pockets of wild birds still living in central Ohio, it's a rare occurrence when the Old Man sees a cockbird standing along a fenceline separating fields that should be full of pheasants. So rare are these sightings in the northeastern corner of Ohio that the Old Man will actually pick up the phone and call me. "You'll never guess what I saw today, Jake," the conversation will start. And 630 miles away, I'll smile, knowing full well that Pop, one more time, caught a glimpse of 1958 in the twenty-first century.

"In the late 1980s," remembers native Iowan Dave Fountain, "it was nothing to go out and get a six-man

This is how many hunters nationwide are introduced to Mister Ringneck. SOUTH DAKOTA TOURISM

limit of roosters by 10:30. And that was most of the time, not just opening week. Hell, we'd laugh at the guys who were still hunting after lunchtime, because you just knew they were doing something wrong," Fountain says with a grin. "There was just nothing like it." And then he, too, fades away into the present. We were eight weeks into the 2004–05 Iowa pheasant season, and Fountain, along with his black Lab, Shadow, had killed a grand total of two roosters. *Two.*

"I just drove the fifteen miles from Anamosa," Fountain, a deputy sheriff, tells me one morning from his cell phone, "and I didn't pass one field in all that way where I thought to myself, 'Man, I'd love to hunt that for pheasants.' I don't know how, but it's changed. Weather, agriculture . . . you missed it, M. D. You should have been here in the 1980s."

Despite appearances, this chapter *is not* about a lack of pheasants. It's about pheasants, and it's about not being able to remember a time when there weren't pheasants in the United States. Looking back on my time in Trumbull County, Ohio, some of those years weren't filled to overflowing with ringnecks. In fact, in the twenty years I spent as an enthusiastic upland hunter in Ohio, I killed but *one* two-bird limit of wild roosters. But that's not my point here. My point is simple: Most of us hunters in the United States can-

not remember a time when the king of the upland, the ring-necked pheasant, wasn't a citizen.

There was a time, however, when the crowing of a spring rooster was absent from the nation's wild audio files. The time was 1880, and the United States was still several months away from having anything remotely resembling a wild ring-necked pheasant population—or a single wild ring-necked pheasant, for that matter. That would change in 1881, thanks to a fellow by the name of Owen Denny. Judge Denny, as he was known to his colleagues, was the U.S. consulate general to Shanghai, China, in the 1880s. Over the course of his trips back and forth to Asia, or so the story goes, Denny developed quite a liking for roast pheasant. As is often the case with men, this hunger served as a catalyst for action. Denny's tastebuds offered all the encouragement he needed, and in 1881 his first shipment of twenty-one Chinese ring-necked pheasants reached the United States via the Oregon shore.

I say "first shipment" somewhat hesitantly, because Denny's successful pheasant importation of 1881 wasn't his original attempt at shipping birds overseas. Unfortunately—or perhaps fortunately for them—the sailors aboard the vessels making those early runs between China and the Pacific Northwest *also* had a fondness for pheasant, since it provided a wonderful reprieve from the daily grind of hardtack, an orange (scurvy, don't you know!), and mutton. Eventually, though, the good judge's box of twenty-one birds reached America intact, and it's to these original twenty-one avian pioneers that we uplanders owe our greatest thanks. Oh, and to Judge Denny, too.

Wild ringnecks were first introduced into Oregon's Willamette Valley, a wonderfully green place lying midway between the Cascades and the coast, and despite what many see as perpetual gloom, rain, and certainly nonpheasant-esque weather, these Chinese newcomers did quite well—so well that within less than ten years, offspring from these original plantings were sent a-packing to Oregon's sister state to the south, California.

In the years to follow, Judge Denny's wonderful gift to the American sportsman would be introduced to and

Judge Denny's original shipment of ringnecks looked no different than this handsome fellow.
SOUTH DAKOTA TOURISM

Regardless of what he's called, there is one common denominator regarding the rooster pheasant: He's challenging.

welcomed across much of the United States. The turning of the page into the twentieth century saw pheasants distributed throughout much of the West—Utah, Colorado, Idaho, Oklahoma, and Texas. Then it was the Midwest's turn, with birds putting down roots in South Dakota, Illinois, Iowa, Indiana, and Ohio. Soon they moved east into Pennsylvania, a state that at one time supported one of the most phenomenal wild pheasant populations in the country. And finally they reached the New England states, where ruffed grouse and woodcock traditionalists slowly—and in some cases, begrudgingly—began to take notice of the ringneck's abilities on the wing and the bird's magnificence on the table. Only in the Southeast, on those lands below the Mason-Dixon Line, and in the Southwest has the ringneck never taken hold (save for some pen-reared cousins and occasional pockets of wild birds).

But that, folks, was then, and this is now. Today those sections of the country—Pacific Northwest, West, Midwest, and East—that played home to the original ringneck settlers still maintain populations of this wondrous gamebird. In some places, especially South Dakota, Iowa, and even portions of Montana and eastern Washington to name but a handful, the ringneck is not only holding its own but is doing quite well. It's not doing as well, unfortunately, as at the turn of the twentieth century, but well nonetheless. In other locales, however, such as the once-pheasant-rich hills of Pennsylvania, the frenzied cackle of a flushing wild rooster is to a large extent a thing of the past. The pheasant is not gone from these places entirely, though, and with luck and the sportsman's helping hand, it never will be. Yet in a small corner of northeastern Ohio, the rarity of the bird's visits have certainly not gone unnoticed.

"I do miss seeing the birds, those pheasants that used to be on your Dzedo's farm," the Old Man will say from time to time, a faraway look in his eyes. "Yep," he'll continue as he turns away, "I always did like chasing those roosters." You, and a lot of other folks, Pop. You and a lot of other folks.

THE RING-NECKED PHEASANT

I'm *not* going to take this opportunity to get scientific with you about the bird we know as the ring-necked pheasant. That doesn't mean I'm going to leave you in the dark about its background, but I'm just not going to cover the pheasant family tree back to a time when the scales on its legs reached from the tips of its toes to the end of its beak.

Above: The white neck "ring" from which the species gets its moniker is plainly visible. SOUTH DAKOTA TOURISM
Right: Iridescent is putting it mildly when it comes to describing a rooster's plumage.

In his wonderful book *The Ring-Necked Pheasant* first published in 1962, the late John Madson told of forty-two species of pheasants in Asia and Asia Minor. Today a search on the Internet will bring up from thirty-five to forty-seven or forty-eight variations, counting the peafowl. But that, folks, is as technical as we're going to get. Here in the American wild, we have but one pheasant. Call it the Chinese pheasant, the ringneck, or, as Mr. Madson did, the ring-necked pheasant. Call it what you will, but it's our bird now, and I know few diehard pheasant hunters who would be willing to give it back.

Okay, perhaps one more technicality. The ring-necked pheasant (*Phasianus colchicus torquatus*) is of the order Galliformes, which translates into "chickenlike." And I'll stop right there, for any further comparison between a wild ring-necked pheasant and your average garden-variety chicken . . . well, I just don't think it shows much respect to the ringneck. Certainly, an old rooster pheasant can be quite the ladies' man, as can a big Rhode Island Red. And yes, I've seen more than one cockbird capable of kicking the tail feathers of any barnyard brawling banty rooster. And all right,

so maybe there *is* just a little visual similarity between a pheasant and—boy, I hate to say this—your ordinary chicken, but I promise we'll stop there.

The Rooster

The male ringneck—called a rooster, cockbird, or cock pheasant—is, as is often but not always the case, the gaudier of the two sexes. He's also the larger, although there can be small roosters and large hens, as is the case with most wild species. Typically, though there will always be variations in the wild, an adult cockbird weighs from two and a half to slightly more than three pounds. Some preserve or pen-raised roosters can tip the scales at around the four-pound mark, but in the wild, a ringneck has to work for a living—enough said.

The rooster's visual appearance offers one of the great mysteries of nature, to which any pheasant hunter who has spent time in the field can attest: How can something as bright and colorful as a rooster pheasant disappear into grass no higher than an ordinary straight pin? That an old cockbird can compress himself as flat as a sheet of notebook paper and hide in cover so short as to make a meadow mouse stick out like a Styrofoam

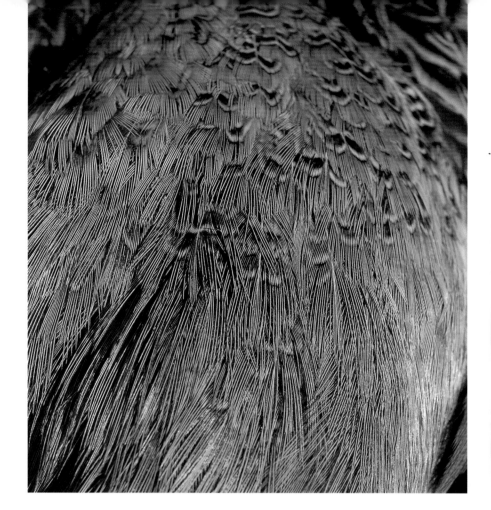

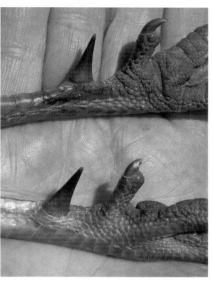

Left: More hairlike than resembling feathers, the plumes on a rooster's back are one of a kind.
Below: Don't think they'll hurt? They're not there for looks, partner.

cup in a coal bin—well, that's just plain incredible. And when he flushes, his tiny pheasant lungs giving it their all, from that "can't be nothing here" clump of bean stubble . . . we'll just see if what you've said about your "nerves of steel" is actually true.

A rooster's ivory or off-white beak or bill is well suited to its task of picking up the seeds, spilled grains, young greens, and insects that make up the bulk of the pheasant's diet. As with any bird, a rooster's beak, though I won't go so far as to call it formidable, may come into play during confrontations between two opposing forces; it's the spurs, however, that serve as the rooster's primary weapon.

Above the cockbird's white neck collar, for which the ringneck was named, his head is a wonderful mix of iridescent purples, blacks, greens, and blues. Around each eye is a heart-shaped red patch, or wattle. These colorful patches, like the patriotic hues on a wild turkey gobbler's head, play a role in both attracting hens and discouraging potential territorial trespassers or rivals. It would seem that for much of his year, a rooster pheasant is either fighting or contributing to the next season's brood. When he is angered

(and I believe roosters get angry) or making amorous advances toward a hen, these red patches become more pronounced, thus adding to that particular bird's intimidation or handsomeness factor. The top of a rooster's head, or crown, is an almost metallic greenish gray, with bright white liners just above the eye separating it from the iridescent blue. Ending an inch or so above the white neck ring, the crown features twin tufts, or ears, as they're often called, which can be raised and lowered at will. They are thought, like the red facial wattles, to play a role in male-to-male confrontations or breeding.

A cockbird's chest is a collection of reddish rusty feathers, like new copper pennies, each tipped in the blackest of blacks. If you've ever seen a rooster standing tall with the sun full on his chest, you know exactly what I mean; it's electric, or very much seems so. The belly is a conglomeration of blacks and metallic blues, with a portion of gold thrown in for good measure; golds and black-tipped golds dominate the upper sides. Farther back, soft, fluffy feathers of subdued hues—browns and grays and whites—cover the rooster's lower sides and thighs.

From above, an adult rooster pheasant is no less handsome than he is viewed from the side or chest. His back and the area just below the white ring is robed in feathers that are a painter's palette of gold and black, reddish brown, and an iridescent green that practically jumps from the bird's body and onto your retina. These colors gradually give way to chestnut browns centered with whites and blacks and, incredibly, the same glowing green as above. The rump is covered with soft greens and blues, complete with circles of muted blacks and whites. These give way to hairlike feathers of reddish brown, greens, soft blues, and an almost yellowish hue. All in all, Mister Cockbird is a wonderfully handsome creature, and if you hold a bird aloft and turn it slightly in the sunlight, you know what it's like to possess the world's largest and most beautiful jewel.

The rooster's wings are drab, with the primaries barred in a gray-white pattern not unlike a gobbler's black-white striping. The remainder of the wings is of a similar gray, with the longer secondaries being somewhat darker and including irregular touches of reddish browns, blacks, and light whites. As for the rooster's famed tail feathers, though the tail often differs from bird to bird, many cockbirds sport eight central tail feathers in four pairs—one pair longest, a second somewhat shorter, and so on. It's the longest set, perhaps twenty-two to twenty-six inches in length, that both grace the successful shooter's candlestick holder and frustrate the one whose focus, incorrectly, is on a flushing rooster's dancing barred trailers and not on his white-ringed neck, as it should be. The central portion of the cock's longest tail feathers is a brilliant gold, which gives way to fringelike muted golds and reds out toward the edges. Striking black bars crisscross each set of tail feathers, but these are most noticeable on the outermost or longest pair.

On their feet, pheasants have three forward toes, each with its own toenail or claw, as well as a hind toe, also with a sharp nail. The legs and feet are a light slate gray from the "knee" (if pheasants have knees) to the slightly darker nails and are scaled, much as were their prehistoric relatives' legs and feet. Just above the hind toe and on the back of the leg is a sharp, bony spur. Varying in shades of black, gray, and even ivory white, these spurs make excellent weapons and are used solely for the purpose of combat. And please trust me on

Male or female? Look close and then look again, particularly during the early season when young roosters (left) might not yet be fully feathered.

this—whether their owner is alive or deceased, a sharp set of spurs can cut you. Should their owner be alive and less than enthused about being in your possession, they can cut you badly. My advice is to use caution when handling a live or dead bird.

Before I move on to his lady friend, I would like to say one more thing about old Mister Cockbird. Early-season roosters aren't always as well dressed as they might become as the season progresses, and this is particularly true of young-of-the-year cocks. During the opening two weeks of the season—hell, for that matter, during the first month of the season—that bird you're sure is a shabbily dressed or immature rooster might just be a hen. The rule here is to look sharp—look sharp again—and if there's any doubt at all, don't pull the trigger. It's that easy.

Missus Ringneck—brown, drab, and wonderfully camouflaged, all for good reason. SOUTH DAKOTA TOURISM

The Hen

Hen pheasants are drab, as plain as plain can be in a Desert Storm camo collection of buffs and light browns, accented slightly with darker browns and dabs of black. Like the rooster, the hen has an ivory white beak and gray legs, with the same blackish gray toenails or claws. In most cases, the hen pheasant lacks spurs; however, a few have them, in the same way that some hen turkeys sport beards.

Since Mama Pheasant is largely responsible for future ringneck populations, it's a good thing that she really doesn't stand out visually. This way, she is less noticeable to things with a hankering for pheasant—hawks, owls, foxes, coyotes, and the like. This lack of conspicuousness becomes even more of a plus during the spring and early summer, when female ringnecks are nesting and raising young broods. Mama Pheasant is wonderfully camouflaged, thanks to Mother Nature.

The hen pheasant is in most cases a devoted, though single, parent. She typically lays eight to twelve eggs per clutch, which she incubates for approximately twenty-three days before hatching. They hatch sometime from early May through the first part of September, depending on geographic location, and other variables such as the weather. All the eggs hatch within two complete turns of the clock, thus not leaving a single kid behind. Once out of the shell, the fuzzy, striped chicks are surprisingly well suited to life in the wild and on their own, though their mother keeps a remarkably close eye on them, even going so far as to attack critters much larger than herself in defense of her little ones. Growing fat on a diet of spiders, bugs, seeds, and other wonderfully nutritious things, the chicks can fly reasonably well at two weeks of age. By two months, they are almost fully feathered and are ready to begin the next stage of their education, a period also known as Hunting Season.

Hens on the wing are easily identified—that is, if you take the time to look.

Evading Predators

Pheasants have three ways of evading predators: They can hide, they can run, and they can fly. And believe me—rooster or hen, it doesn't matter—these birds are masters of all three techniques.

Hiding: If you think about it for a minute, it makes perfect sense that it would be easy for the hen pheasant to hide. Drab brown and mottled with Mother Nature's shadows, she is difficult to see in most natural settings. She simply blends in, as she's supposed to do. A cockbird, on the other hand, should stand out vividly, and yet he too is a master of the disappearing act. Couple this knack for getting invisible with the pheasant's habit of sitting tight and letting both man and beast wander right by, and if you're anything like me, you really start to wonder just how many pheasants you've passed for every one you've actually seen. If you knew the truth, you likely would be downright ashamed of yourself.

"Pheasants didn't used to run," native Iowan Dave Fountain tells me several times each season. "We never used blockers. The rooster that ran out of gun range and flushed at 150 yards was the exception, not the rule. But that's not the way it is today," he says none too happily. "Hell, these roosters aren't any different than the Huns we'll sometimes see. You're lucky if those Huns will land in the same section you're hunting. These roosters? They'll flat run out of the time zone."

I've seen more times than not when Mr. Fountain was right—roosters do dearly love to run, perhaps more now than they did thirty or forty years ago, and there are plenty of people with plenty of theories why. One is simple: We've killed all the roosters that fly, leaving only those that run. It's a genetic thing, proponents of the runners-breed-runners brigade will tell you. Do I believe it? I don't think so, though on any given day the theory certainly can make sense or at least give you something to think about.

I'm more prone, however, to believe this run-versus-fly situation has more to do with changing farming practices than it does the survival of the fittest. You see, there was a time "back when" when fencerows and waterways were agriculturally unruly. Cornfields weren't like they are today, with nary a strand of foxtail

Though often he'd rather run, an old rooster is no slouch when it comes to getting airborne. SOUTH DAKOTA TOURISM

or goldenrod. The cover was wide and thick and abundant, and the roosters couldn't see you coming a half-section away. They felt safe surrounded by everything wild, and they opted, "back when," for options one and three; that is, they hid or flew. Or they hid then flew. Today, however, fencerows (if they exist) are often no wider than a razor's edge. Waterways are often mown as short as a fairway, and the ground under standing corn is devoid of anything resembling a weed.

What's my point? I subscribe to three different theories on why pheasants today would rather run than fly. I realize that a person should have but one true belief as to why something does or doesn't happen, but this is my book, and being somewhat indecisive and certainly no wildlife biologist, I choose to have three.

First, there's the *cover theory*. This idea is based on the fact that in many cases, today's pheasant cover could only be described as thin or sparse as compared

to, say, thirty years ago. Given thick and therefore secure cover, pheasants were more likely to hunker, hide, and hope that you'd walk past. If you would stop, they'd get nervous and flush. Or your black Lab would stick its nose under that old rooster's tail feathers and he'd flush. Pheasants don't feel as secure in today's marginal cover and opt instead to put as much space— call it "pseudo-cover"—as they possibly can between themselves and a potential predator, namely you. But, you ask, what about a farm that still has good cover, like it was back when. I'm talking switchgrass, foxtail, and goldenrod, cover the likes of which we see in David Maas's paintings. These birds still run. Why?

Perhaps here it's the *exposure theory* that comes into play. A pheasant in the air has exposed itself 100 percent to the possibility of personal tragedy, whether that tragedy comes as a result of lead pellets, a hawk or eagle, a tree limb, a power line, or what have you.

The Old Man in all his glory. SOUTH DAKOTA TOURISM

Surrounded by nothing but open space, a pheasant is most vulnerable. At the risk of personifying this wild creature, I believe that intermediate members of the food chain such as pheasants realize or recognize (notice I did not say "understand") those instances when they are most vulnerable or exposed to harm. That said, a pheasant then instinctively chooses that self-protective measure that least exposes it to danger. Translation: It runs.

The *population and perception theory* has direct ties to the *exposure theory*. The *population and perception theory* suggests that pheasants have always run from danger, and as long as humans have presented themselves as a dangerous sort, pheasants have run from them. Where things change, though, is with the current pheasant population. Take Ohio in 1958. Someone could hunt all season long and see perhaps one hundred wild pheasants total. Of these birds, fifty would run and flush wide or simply run, though seen, and never flush. The remaining fifty, then, would hold and play the game as they should. Say that roughly one-third of these birds—seventeen—were roosters, and the hunter killed eight.

Jump ahead to 2005. The original hunter's son, working top-notch ground in the central and north-central parts of the state, sees throughout the season only thirty-five wild pheasants. Eighteen of these birds run; seventeen fly. Six of these fliers are cockbirds, and the young man manages to scratch down half of those.

The proportion of runners to fliers hasn't changed from 1958 to 2005; in fact, none of the proportions changed at all in the forty-seven years between father and son. What did change was overall pheasant populations—but to the young hunter in the twenty-first century, it would appear that damn near every pheasant is a runner.

The Haunts

Although I'll discuss what constitutes pheasant cover much more in-depth in the chapter on tactics, and habitat to a greater extent in the chapter on the pheasant's future, I just want to take a minute and talk about cover in relation to the calendar—where you're likely to find pheasants at any given time during the year.

Spring: Scientific research it's not, but the majority of the pheasants I see while hunting gobblers in the spring are using what I'll—again, unscientifically—refer to as thin cover: roadside spike rushes, lighter stands of reed canary grass, sumac with short grasses, early emerging grain crops such as corn or soybeans, and the like. Perhaps it's because of the bugs found in these places, a welcome feast after the slim pickings of weeks past. Maybe it's the advent of nicer weather. Or, and I'm prone to follow this line of thinking, the roosters may prefer this more open type of cover because it provides an open-air stage from which they can attract multitudinous hens. Nighttime roosting cover may still be heavier: cattails, set-aside acres, thicker waterways, treed shelterbelts. Hens also may be gravitating toward this heavier cover as nesting time approaches.

Summer: Warm weather prevails across pheasant country. The hens are taking their chicks on daily walkabouts in search of bugs, and this means short-grass fields, timber edges, and taller cropfields. Mornings and evenings, you'll see the families alongside gravel roads, picking and dusting. To a large extent, the roosters have gone solitary, wandering nomadically around their relatively small home ranges. Roosting cover hasn't changed, but the options now are much broader as warmer temperatures and June rains cause the grass to grow quickly.

Fall: In late September and early October, wherever there's corn, chances are good you'll find pheasants. Standing corn has everything the roosters, hens, and near-adult young-of-the-year birds need: clear running at ground level, overhead cover, grit, occasional water, and a good supply of bugs. It's damn near perfect. Where there's no corn, overgrown fencelines bordering ground in production are a good bet, as are weedy draws and transition areas between cropfields and heavy cover such as cattails. This time of year, the cover's as good as it's going to get, food's plentiful, and the birds are scattered. Come opening day, you'll likely find roosters anywhere.

Winter: Though pheasants often hunker down in heavy cover, in winter it doesn't necessarily mean you'll find them only in the thickest, nastiest stuff that God ever created. That can be the case, but on a sunny 25-degree day in late December with no wind, you're going to find me working the lighter cover—higher bromegrass, high-cut corn stubble, thin creek

Life's easy for this hen during the summer; winter might be a different story.

Fall and a rooster pheasant are synonymous terms in many parts of the country. SOUTH DAKOTA TOURISM

bottoms. Why? Because like me, the birds take advantage of the nice weather to sun themselves, stretch their legs, and fill their bellies. As soon as the weather turns crummy again, I'll return to the frozen cattail swamps, head-high switchgrass, and once-timbered woodlots overgrown with thigh-high reed canary grass—with not one, but two black Labs in tow. This, folks, is when pheasant hunting *really* gets interesting.

Winter in eastern Iowa is prime time for hunters, their hounds, and the hardy ring-necked pheasant.

Above: Trappers play a principal role in managing pheasant predators, such as the old raccoon lying here on the tailgate.
Right: Red foxes will readily help themselves to a meal of pheasant—eggs, chicks, and adults—should one present itself.

THE PREDATORS

There's a good chance that if you're reading this, you're a pheasant hunter. And if you're a pheasant hunter, there's an equally good chance that you enjoy pheasant on the table. If so, welcome to the club. I like to eat pheasant; in fact, I like pheasant perhaps best of all the wild gamebirds we put in the freezer each year, grouse included. But that said, you and I aren't the only ones who enjoy a meal of fine, white-breasted wild ringneck. Lots and lots of other creatures sharing that same piece of pheasant cover would be happy to sit down to a snack of rooster or hen. And who might these critters be? Let me introduce some of them.

Birds

Hawks and owls certainly won't hesitate to swoop down upon any unwary ringneck they might encounter. Since moving to Iowa in 1997, I'm always amazed come harvest time in October. Up until then, red-tailed hawks are common but not overly abundant. However, once the corn's gone—and I mean within hours of any cornfield being harvested—there's a red-tailed hawk sitting on each locust post and in every dead elm tree along that perimeter of that field. Now don't think that I believe those redtails have shown up solely for the purpose of decimating the local pheasant population; in fact, it's the field mice, rats, and cottontails that take the brunt of this annual aerial attack. But that said, I'm

sure there are plenty of ringnecks that fall under the talented talons of these airborne predators. Owls, too, particularly our largest common owl, the great horned, can play hell with pheasant population. Surprisingly, these winged meat eaters account for a very small portion of the actual predation on pheasants. Rabbits, on the other hand, aren't so lucky.

Most folks don't realize that crows also have an impact on wild animal populations, particularly other birds. Eggs and chicks both are on their regular menu. Many times I've watched crows, usually in pairs, harass a nest sitter to the point of driving it off the nest so they might fly off with their prize. Sheds an entirely new light on the sport of crow hunting, eh?

Canines and Felines

Of all potential pheasant predators, I believe I'm safe in saying that foxes and coyotes get the most attention and have the worst reputation. However, every biologist I've talked with, every knowledgeable pheasant hunter I've known, and every study I've looked at seems to indicate that these wild canines are much more likely to fill their furry bellies with rodents such as meadow mice, squirrels, chipmunks, and cottontails. But should a roving fox or coyote stumble across a sitting hen pheasant, it's probably not going to pass up an easy meal. (Honestly, would you turn your back on a free six-pack and a pepperoni pizza?)

Coyote hunting enthusiast Chad Belding of Avery Outdoors lends a helping hand to the Utah pheasant population.
CHAD BELDING

Feral or unsupervised dogs and house cats often are tremendous killers of wildlife, pheasants included. Studies done in Great Britain have shown that house-cats, both feral and domestic, are responsible for the death of hundreds of thousands, if not millions, of songbirds each year. Trust me, a tabby that spends half its time roaming the fields when it's not sleeping in the garage isn't going to make a distinction between a rufous-sided towhee and a month-old rooster pheasant. Dogs, too, can be terribly hazardous to the health of a pheasant population, particularly in the spring, when hens and their little ones are most vulnerable. So if you have a dog or cat, always make sure it's supervised, indoors, kenneled, or otherwise unable to harm wild animal populations. If you see what you consider to be wild or feral dogs or cats while in the field, report them immediately to the local sheriff's department or animal control agency. I'm not a cat fan, and I'm not going to endorse any particular action, though not everyone feels the same way. A good friend of mine follows the "quarter-mile rule." If, Dave says, a cat in the field is within a quarter-mile of an occupied residence, it's safe. More than a quarter-mile? I'll let you draw your own conclusions.

Other Mammals

Skunks, opossums, and raccoons are major problems when it comes to pheasant predation, especially on eggs. One solution is trapping. If, as was done in Washington in 2000, the people of your state attempt to prohibit trapping via the ballot box, fight them with every resource at your disposal. The active trapper is one of the wild pheasant's best friends.

Humans

One human source of pheasant mortality is regulated hunting and the associated kill. Wildlife biologists establish guidelines for the harvest of the species that are intended to be nondetrimental to the pheasant population. So though hunting is indeed a human-related source of pheasant mortality, the losses within the population as a result of hunting are acceptable. Also, hunters targeting wild pheasant populations are harvesting roosters only. Since cockbirds are notoriously polygamous, it takes but one rooster to service a parcel of hens.

Mowing is another cause of mortality, particularly in spring and early summer, when hens are incubating eggs and are extremely reluctant to leave their nests. If only the clutch of eggs is destroyed by a John Deere or Massey-Ferguson, this is not so disastrous, as most hens will renest should their first attempt prove futile. But when both clutch *and* hen are lost under a mower's blades . . . well, that's a total loss. In some years and in some states, such mower mortality can be considerably, if not alarmingly, high. Over the years, many different things have been tried to decrease pheasant losses due to mowing. Flushing bars—steel bars with dangling chains attached to one side of the machinery that flush birds from their nests prior to the machine's next deadly round—save hens, yet the nests are still destroyed. And the problem with flushing bars is that they have to be installed and maintained in order to function as designed. In my thirty years of being around farms, I've never seen a flushing bar in use. Hell, for that matter, I've never seen a flushing bar, except in pictures. I don't have an answer, and I'm certainly not going to point a finger at the American farmer, who already has more than his fair share of hurdles to contend with. Delaying mowing as long into the spring as possible is another option; however, a farmer can let his alfalfa or hay get only so high before something has to be done with it. The bottom line is that as long as pheasants nest in cover both supplied and manipulated by humans using sharp, rapidly rotating blades, there is going to be resulting pheasant mortality.

I'd probably be remiss here if I didn't mention something, albeit briefly, about automobiles. Surprisingly enough, even in a state like Iowa, with a relatively substantial pheasant population, I seldom see birds that have been killed as a result of an encounter with a Ford, Chevrolet, or Dodge. I won't go so far as to say it's rare to see a road-killed pheasant, but it's certainly not as everyday an occurrence as are flattened skunks, raccoons, or opossums. Oddly, probably 75 percent or so of the pheasants I see killed at the edge of the road are hens. Is that because there are more hens in most pheasant populations? Or because the hens aren't as afraid of playing in traffic as are the roosters? I would imagine there's a reason, but it seems to be known only to the birds themselves. With that, let it suffice to say that automobiles can definitely impact a pheasant population—literally.

Another cause of pheasant mortality can be attributed to both humans and Mother Nature. As is the case with all wild creatures, Mother Nature can be a terrible witch when it comes to pheasants. Though more than capable of fending for themselves, pheasants can suffer from the effects of severe or prolonged cold, snowfall, ice, drought, wet—essentially, any climatic conditions above and beyond what might be considered normal. Given suitable habitat that provides not only cover for protection such as brush, trees, switchgrass, cattails, or sage, but access to adequate food and water, the harm from these extreme conditions to wild pheasant populations can be greatly lessened. Severe weather can result in increased pheasant mortality, but with good cover, this mortality can be kept to a level that does not affect long-term pheasant numbers. It's actually quite simple: Give them a decent place to live, and wild pheasants will do just fine on their own. Take away that habitat, as humans do with thousands of suitable acres each year, and not only do pheasants suffer, but so do all wild animal populations.

In healthy pheasant populations, hunting has little effect on the overall welfare of the birds.

Snow and ice can impact pheasant populations dramatically, particularly when suitable winter cover is lacking.

CHAPTER 2

Strategies and Tactics

"If he's going to run like a rabbit, I'm going to shoot him like a rabbit."

YES, SIR, THAT'S WHAT MY POP SAID YEARS ago. And before any of you start wringing your hands and condemning me, my Pop, our beagles, and anyone who would ever think of ground-swatting a rooster, let me remind you that this comment was a carryover from the man's formative years in the late 1940s and early 1950s. The pheasants that he might have shot on the farm whose feet were still on the ground went to help feed a family of six kids, his mom, and my Dzedo—Slovak for grandfather. Sporting? Perhaps not by today's standards, or even back then; however, there was nothing particularly sporting about being hungry either. Am I justifying the actions? Probably; maybe not. It was his decision and his belly, and those of his brothers and sisters. 'Nough said about that.

There are, I'm sure, 101 ways to shoot a rooster pheasant. Actually, there are probably more, and if I wanted to be extremely accurate, I would change "shoot" to "corner, attempt to flush into the air, and then bring to earth via a charge from one's trusty fowling piece." Or something like that.

In its most elemental form, pheasant hunting involves walking around likely looking pheasant habitat, aka cover, until a bird flushes. Should it be a rooster, the hunter takes the shot. If it's a hen, the shot is passed up unless it's in a preserve setting where hens

A successful end to a well-thought-out strategy. PHIL BOURJAILY

are fair game. Such an outing typically involves one, two, or sometimes more folks, though in some settings, larger groups gather. In South Dakota, for example, you might see an avian assault with eight or ten walkers and a similar number of standers, blockers, or posters—whatever you want to call them. Often canine assistance in the form of a pointing or flushing dog is thrown into the mix, the dog's role being to find, flush, and retrieve the harvested birds.

The setting for any pheasant hunt can differ, not only from state to state, but also among areas within a state or even a county, township, or section. In Iowa, within a few minutes' walk, I can probe into a range of cover types: thick matted cattail marshes, rolling hills covered with bromegrass, damn near impenetrable tangles in creek bottoms or plum thickets, and chest-high switchgrass—but we'll get to that in a minute.

Before we consider strategies and tactics in earnest, I want to say something that probably needn't be said . . . and I will word this carefully. As long as an individual's chosen technique for hunting pheasants is legal within the guidelines and regulations set forth by the state fish and game agency, then it is a legitimate method. You might not agree with the concept of road hunting—driving the rural gravel roads until a rooster is spotted and then climbing out of the rig, loading the shotgun, and jumping the bird out of the road ditch. You might not agree with watching a piece of roosting cover just before sunrise, hoping to pass-shoot, for lack of a better phrase, an old cockbird on his way to bed for the evening. Your method of choice (and your *only* method of choice) may be gunning ringnecks one-on-one with a trusty English setter and shooting at only those birds that your pup has skillfully pointed.

Lee Harstad and Maggie take a breather during a South Dakota hunt on ground overlooking the Missouri River.

The author, helped by Jet and Deacon, works the cattails during a mid-December Iowa outing.

Some strategies, such as hunting with a pointing dog, are perhaps viewed as being more sporting than others, such as road hunting and using standers or blockers. But such techniques are rooted in tradition and who are we to say that these traditions are wrong so long as they are legal? My point is simple: different strokes for different folks, as long as it's done safely and legally and with an eye on the reputation of every hunter who takes up sporting arms in the fall, for we are all representatives of the pheasant hunting tradition.

RULE NUMBER ONE—BE QUIET

From an educational standpoint, it was a classic hunt. On a frustration scale of one to ten . . . well, let's just say it was a learning experience.

The phone rang one evening in December. "M. D., it's Joey," said the voice on the other end. Joey was a young man, maybe sixteen, and an aspiring upland bird hunter. Unfortunately, Joey knew little about upland bird hunting, hence the telephone call. "Hey," he said, the excitement clearly evident, "I got permission to hunt a piece of ground just north of Springville. There's

lots of pheasants, but I don't know what I'm doing. And I don't have a dog." (The kid was honest, I'll certainly give him that.) "Would you be interested in taking me tomorrow morning? We're off school for Christmas break, and I'd really like to get a pheasant. Oh, and could you bring Maggie?" Maggie was my black Lab. Behind the handset, I grinned. Sure, I told him, I'd pick him up at 8, and we'd be hunting shortly after. And yes, I'd bring Maggie. He thanked me 142 times in machine-gun fashion and hung up. Running, I'm sure, to make certain his stuff was all in order.

I picked up Joey the next morning, and we made the short drive out to the field he had permission to hunt. From the gravel road at the gate entry, I could see a wide, weedy creek bottom with several equally rugged high-grass waterways heading out in different directions. A larger creek bordered by tall cottonwoods formed the western boundary of the place, and on all sides, cut cornfields stretched as far as the eye could see. It certainly looked good from a pheasant stand-point. All this and three or four inches of relatively new snow on the ground, and I was smiling as I braked the

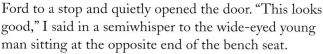

Above: Discussing the plan is fine, but can you do it quietly?
Right: Nebraska's Dana Douglas prefers to do his bird
hunting from horseback, a novel approach in today's
internal-combustion-oriented world.

Ford to a stop and quietly opened the door. "This looks good," I said in a semiwhisper to the wide-eyed young man sitting at the opposite end of the bench seat.

Pheasants living outside of Cedar Rapids, Iowa, get smart in a hurry. Come late December, these birds—at least those that haven't had the pleasure of riding back to town in someone's truck—have been through two hunter-heavy holidays and damn near a dozen weekends. Those that have survived the onslaught are incredibly nervous.

BAM! Joey, who had opened his door silently enough, apparently wanted to make sure he shut it sufficiently. "LOOK! M. D., look. There's a bird! And there's another!" And the boy was right. There were two pheasants, flying, not surprisingly, at a rapid rate of speed toward the damn-near-impenetrable cover of the wooded creek bottom. These birds, roosters both, were soon joined by half a dozen others, then six more, then a dozen, and on and on and on until the half section we had *planned* to hunt looked like a black undulating wave . . . a wave of pheasants escaping.

In the backseat, Maggie whined, a desperate "Let me the hell out of here so I can chase those things!"

kind of deep-throated whimper. I understood the sound all too well. I had failed. I had failed Maggie and I had failed Joey. I had forgotten to mention the one rule, the Rule Above All Others, concerning late-season pheasants: Be quiet.

"I did that, didn't I," Joey finally broke the silence, this time with a small, almost timid voice instead of a seventy-five-pound truck door. "I probably shouldn't have slammed the door, huh?" No longer concerned about being quiet, I let Maggie loose, walked around, and slapped the boy on the shoulder. "Ah," I told him, "we may find one down there somewhere. A deaf one, maybe." And I smiled. Joey smiled back. Lesson learned, I thought, as I shrugged into my vest and grabbed my over/under out of its case, Joey doing the same. That's the neat thing about pheasants: There are always lessons to be learned.

Safety is priority one, regardless of the species hunted; that should go without saying. But when it comes to pheasants, being quiet is the most important rule that must be adhered to. The noisy hunter who hits the field slamming vehicle doors and shotgun bolts, yelling at his dog for the first of a million times that morning, and generally making a ruckus may see and actually shoot a few birds—deaf ones, I suppose. But the quiet, stealthy hunter will be able to get up close and personal with pheasants that the noisy one simply won't see.

When it comes to pheasants, quiet is very elemental. Can you park your rig someplace where it can be neither seen nor heard? Remember, roosters have eyes as well as ears. A cockbird that sees you, your orange hat, and your big truck will run just as readily as one that hears you. If a walk is necessary before the hunt actually begins, can you do so quietly and, to some extent, unseen? Will your dog behave and walk at heel until you're ready to go, or is yours one of those yelling-at hounds—you know, the type that roosters dearly love to see hit the field? Pheasant hunting, especially late season been-through-the-grinder pheasant hunting, can be all about strategy. And as you continue on here in this section, remember that many, if not all, of these strategies have hunting quiet as their foundation.

HUNTING SOLO

For many, pheasant hunting is a social affair—something like dove hunting, only with a lot more walking and a whole lot more blaze orange. And there's absolutely nothing wrong with this. I'm not a huge fan of the large-group style of pheasant hunting, however, and I don't do much group hunting, regardless of the species. Though I have had some very enjoyable pheasant outings where I was one of many, there's just something about hunting solo when it comes to ringnecks—something that only the one-on-one aspect provides.

Roosters, regardless of the time of year, are a tremendously worthy adversary. Every time I head afield by my lonesome and manage somehow to tuck a cockbird into my game vest, I really feel as though I've accomplished something. With an early-January rooster who's seen more than his fair share of gun-toting humans, my chest swells a little bigger. Call it the "David and Goliath Syndrome" or the "Indians Win the Series Syndrome"—I call it feelin' good.

Assuming that cover with birds is indeed part of your mix, successfully hunting roosters on your own—without the help of a hound—involves four key components: go small, go smart, go slow, and stop often. Now, let's take a look at each of these.

Go Small

Going small refers to evaluating your hunting ground and cutting it, if necessary, into sections or parcels that can truly be managed by a single hunter. Depending on the cover, this may be one acre or ten or fifty. My point is that too large a hunting area leaves the birds far too many avenues of escape. You simply can't cover it all. And though the roosters may not recognize these opportunities in the way a human would, they will nonetheless take advantage of these unguarded escape routes to get away.

Go Smart

As you decide how to cut your hunting property into manageable sections, think about *how* you're going to hunt these sections. It's important to understand

In many instances, going solo is the best option—it's quiet, it's elemental, and it works.

The author and Jet walk a small section of heavy cover hoping to push birds to the edge of the agricultural ground.

a couple of key points about pheasants and pheasant hunting. First, roosters—actually, pheasants in general—will typically fly from thinner cover to areas of heavier cover. Say, for instance, you're walking through a wonderfully semi-soggy combination of foxtail and goldenrod interspersed with small tangles of short cattails. On your left are several acres of eight- to ten-inch bromegrass; on your right, chest-high switchgrass. Or maybe it's standing corn . . . it really doesn't matter. What does matter is that any birds you flush from the moderate cover you're walking through are more likely to head for the safety of the tall stuff than they are the bromegrass. What's this mean? You'd better shoot straight on the initial flush, because your chances of a solitary reflush from out of the tall stuff aren't all that good.

Go Slow

The formula here is an elemental one: The faster you go, the more roosters you're going to walk by; that is, the more roosters are going to let you walk by. Remem-

ber what I've said previously. Flying seems to be more of a last resort than a necessity for most of today's cockbirds. If you're moving fast, particularly if you're dogless, you are but a minor inconvenience to many pheasants. They'll simply sit and let you walk right on by. Is there a remedy? Sure—slow down. If I had a dollar . . . hell, if I had two bits (that's twenty-five cents for you young guys) for every time the Old Man told me to slow down, I'd have enough folding money for a three-bedroom, two-bath place in Grosse Point, Michigan.

Stop Often

For the lone gunner, slowing down is just part of the equation. You also need to stop every now and then. To enjoy the scenery? Maybe that's part of it, but by stopping every few steps you make that doesn't-want-to-fly rooster nervous. Really, really nervous. Common theory holds that a prey animal such as a pheasant hearing the repetitive footsteps of a predator will often hold tight in hopes that the predator will walk past. And it works. But let those footfalls stop and the situation changes.

The soloist can greatly improve his success simply by slowing down and stopping often.

Mister Ringneck senses that maybe it has been seen, that maybe it better move, or maybe it should even fly. How many times have you and a gunning partner stopped in the shade to catch your breath and give old Rover a drink, only to have a rooster flush nearby a full minute or two later? And not only with ringnecks, but with ruffed grouse, woodcock, bobwhites, and other upland birds as well. So it's really quite simple—slow down and stop every once in a while.

GROUP HUNTS: WALKERS AND BLOCKERS

Years ago, pheasant hunters borrowed from the pages of the deer hunters' notebooks and began conducting what are essentially pheasant drives. Sure, uplanders call it "posting blockers," but there is very little difference between the two strategies.

In the type of group hunt I'll call "walkers and blockers," you find two distinct roles. The walkers (or the drivers) slowly push pheasants toward some type of cover break—a topographical feature such as a dirt road, clean field, or treeline, or like—that might prompt a rooster or roosters to take to the air. The blockers, also referred to as the shooters, wait, arms at the ready, at this cover break. No cover break? That really poses no problem because the blocker's role is actually a dual role—he's a shooter and a pseudo-cover break. Lacking some type of feature that will force pheasants to take flight, the presence of the blockers can often be enough to put the birds into the air. If not, the blockers cut off the birds' running route, thus keeping them on the ground long enough for the walkers to advance and flush them.

This walk-and-block strategy is actually quite simple and can be very effective, particularly later in the season, when the birds that have survived the first six weeks are legging it out even as you put the key in that old pickup's ignition. However, let's discuss an aspect or two of the walk-and-block method that are important to consider.

Technique, not the number of hunters, is most important. The walk-and-block tactic can work just as well with three guns as it can with thirty. What

Battle lines are drawn prior to the first drive of the morning. Will it work? We'll soon see.

A walker gets a safe shot at a bird that flies away from the line of blockers.

One down, several more to go. Here, the blockers prepare to relocate while the walkers turn around for another push.

Above: Who said anything about walking?
Right: Mark Chestnut stands guard at the end of a strip-cut cornfield in central South Dakota. No birds on this drive, only jackrabbits.

matters is the bite you take out of the cover—match the size of your army to the size of the cover. For instance, you and two pals are going to be hard-pressed to use the push-and-stand method effectively on an eighty-acre patch of switchgrass. A four-acre parcel, on the other hand, would be much more man-ageable. Surround that same four-acre piece with twelve blockers and twelve walkers, and I'm willing to bet that those birds aren't going to tolerate all the inevitable commotion you and your twenty-three cohorts are going to make getting into position. To

use a fly-fishing analogy, it's a case of "matching the hatch." It's also critical that both standers and walkers get into position as quietly as possible.

Later in this chapter you're going to encounter a section on pheasant hunting safety that includes a small section on the safety aspects of this particular hunting method. Read it, because hunting in groups presents unique hazards. It's perfectly acceptable for both walkers and blockers to shoot during the course of such a push, but it needs to be done responsibly, ethically, and following a certain set of rules.

Above: I'm saying it's time to go, but are the roosters on the same schedule?
Left: Anticipation runs high during a drive, especially as the walkers approach the end. Everyone safe?

BY THE CLOCK

Call me lazy if you must, but one of the things I enjoy most about pheasant hunting is the fact that I don't have to get up at 3 A.M. I get enough of that during turkey season, thanks. In fact, some states set a time before which you can't legally hunt. In South Dakota, it's noon and changes to 10 A.M. later in the season. In Iowa, starting time is 8:00 A.M. sharp. While I was growing up in Ohio, the bell rang at 9. I like those times, which make me seriously rethink my policy of not eating breakfast.

Pheasant hunting is one of those consumptive activities that can be good any time of the day. It's true, yes, that the birds often have routines that take them here at this time and there at that time. And it's likewise true that you can take advantage of this routine, but that's not to say that an hour before or after, if it still falls within legal shooting times, can't be just as good.

A rooster's fall schedule is dictated by his stomach, the weather, and seasonal hunting pressure. But in the fall, given pleasant conditions, he gets up, gets something to eat and drink, loafs, gets something else to eat and drink, and goes to roost. As the days get shorter, the times when he does these things change, but the routine stays pretty much the same. Inclement weather, on the other hand, often alters the routine. Rain or snow may keep a cockbird on the roost later and cause him to feed more often with less loafing. Intense hunting pressure can impact a bird's daily walk-through, leading to birds feeding at first light or before legal shooting hours and then leaving the area for some sort of refuge, flying to an adjoining property, a suburban backyard, impenetrable cover— somewhere where you can't get to them. Later that day, as the light fails, they'll return to roost unless late-day hunting pressure keeps them away, a situation that can and does happen.

Though pheasant hunting can be good at any time of day, you should take into consideration the above three variables of stomach, weather, and hunting pressure when deciding both when and where to venture into the field. On a very warm, dry opener, focus on water sources as early as you can legally be in the field. The days are long now, and given pleasant conditions, a rooster's morning begins not long after daybreak. It's dry and though pheasants can go for a time without food, they need water on a daily basis. This means you're likely to find birds near water early, particularly if you can find a food-water mix, such as a cut silage field alongside a creek or a mown winter wheatfield with a seep spring in one shaded corner. That's where you should head first. During chilly rain, roosting cover heads up the list, some place like a brushy hedge (Osage orange) thicket that combines overhead cover with ground-level roosting options. Pheasants don't like to get wet, and on damp, chilly days, they're not

Public ground can also be productive ground, particularly late in the season when the birds bunch up and the hunting pressure drops to near nothing.

likely to wander far from the roost very early, so you can sleep a bit or get some work done first thing in the morning. When it's cold, say 30 degrees with six inches of new snow, you can take your time in the morning, as the birds are probably going to stay on a good roost a little longer than normal; doing so helps conserve vital calories. When they do arise, feeding on high-energy grains such as waste corn is going to be their first activity. A place like a cattail swamp alongside a cut cornfield would be ideal.

ON PUBLIC LANDS

For this topic, I called upon good friend and fellow writer Phil Bourjaily, who pens a monthly shooting column for *Field & Stream* magazine, for his words of wisdom. The consummate pheasant hunter, Bourjaily spends 90 percent or more of his Iowa-based upland time on public ground, and he and his setter Ike do quite well. In past seasons, he and Ike have averaged a bird or slightly more per public land outing, a good number when you consider the amount of pressure that most Iowa public parcels receive throughout pheasant season. But I'm not surprised at Phil's average. He does several important things that, when combined, can lead to success on public land: He hunts smart, he hunts over a good dog, he hunts when others won't, and he makes the most of every shooting opportunity—that is, he's very good with a shotgun.

One rainy afternoon in late August I called Phil and asked him one question: What is the key to success for public-land pheasants? "Low expectations never hurt," he said with a laugh. "If I kill one bird, I'm delighted. I'm not looking for a limit when I hunt public land, especially land here in central Iowa that sees a lot of pressure. But I do enjoy it if I can go out on public land and kill a bird that hasn't cost me a dime, one that's been hunted hard, then I really feel as though I've done something."

But back to my question—the key to success? "It's all about timing," Bourjaily said without skipping a beat. "Now, that's easy to say, but sometimes hard to do. Timing can mean a couple things. One, keep your eye on the harvest. A lot of times, the crops on public land come out after the crops on nearby private lands have been harvested. This means that now the standing corn that provided escape cover is gone, and those birds are vulnerable. That's important—vulnerability."

I'm going to emphasize Bourjaily's "keep your eye on the harvest recommendation" and add one word: *closely*. Try to hunt the evening or morning after that public corn is harvested. You're probably not the only one keeping a close eye on the combines, so get there as early as possible.

"Timing also refers to when you hunt," Bourjaily continued. "Go early in the season when the birds are new. Or if there's a portion of a refuge that opens to pheasant hunting later in the season, be one of the first ones there. Go when the weather's bad—rain, snow, ice, cold. In many instances, the best cover is on the public ground, and while the birds may be on the adjoining private land during the day, they'll come back to the best roosting areas at night. So go early. Or stay late. And hunt with a good dog."

Bourjaily's message is that lazy, fair-weather hunters are going to kill few public land roosters. A handful of birds here and there may earn themselves a ride in the back of a C. C. Filson vest, but those unwary birds will get weeded out in very short order after the season begins. As for the veteran cockbirds, they're a cagy bunch. They'll give you gray hairs and make you think twice about that new blood pressure medication you're taking. But when you kill one you'll understand what Bourjaily meant when he said, "You've really done something there."

THE FORGOTTEN COVERS

In many pheasant-hunting states, large groups of hunters and large parcels of ground are the norm. But the group method and acreages in the double digits aren't the only means to bag a limit of cockbirds. Some of the hottest pheasant hunting falls not to the orange-clad hoards, but to solos or pairs of hunters who concentrate instead on what I'll refer to as *forgotten cover*.

Step One: Reprogramming

This involves rethinking your pheasant-hunting methods and living by a couple of inverse relationships. The first of these is *big means small*. Each January when stories about the biggest bucks harvested emerge, it quickly becomes obvious that many of these deer were taken by gunners or archers working very small parcels of ground. As with deer, pheasants often prefer the smallest, seemingly most insignificant hideouts. This becomes especially true in cases where hunting pres-

Overlook nothing is one of the cardinal rules of pheasant hunting.

sure forces birds into smaller—translation: overlooked—hiding places.

The second of these inverse relationships is *easy means hard.* Nowhere does this statement hold more true than in the case of hunters working large set-aside fields or standing corn early in the season. Unless provided the support of a small army of blaze orange-wearing walkers and blockers, hunters opting to work these challenging habitats often learn a lesson in futility.

Step Two: Definition

The hunter who knows his quarry stands a better chance of being successful from a harvest standpoint. But it's often not enough simply to know one's quarry intimately. In the case of small-cover cockbirds, it's helpful to know just exactly what constitutes small cover.

While opinions differ, I'll define small covers as any type of cover that 99 percent of the competition will overlook. Most hunters won't even consider this ground in the first place simply because it's too small and insignificant. This includes fringe areas, some of the best places to find runaway roosters after the opening bell sounds. Fringe areas exist everywhere and provide some of the most consistent shooting on public hunting areas, where most hunters set their sights on the biggest block of cover on the property. Here fringe areas often consist of a timber-and-brush mixture where fields meet the trees. This same mix can be found on thousands of private parcels around the country, where it can provide equally phenomenal gunning opportunities.

It's important to remember that pheasants will hide in any cover, big or small. Early in the season, when

A gunner tries his hand at a long bird that flushed on the edge where public and private lands meet in northeastern South Dakota.

the weather doesn't dictate heavier cover, roosters will commonly spend time in thin, almost see-through fencelines—areas that won't harbor a single bird come late December. Corn stubble, too, can be extremely attractive in the early season and is commonly overlooked by hunters focusing on nearby waist-high weeds. Stubble or stalks mixed with even the slightest bit of foxtail or ragweed creates a pheasant mecca, a hot spot that can be even better later in the morning once the birds have left their night-roosting cover for the lighter cover and convenient feeding opportunities offered by the corn.

I found a long-spurred cockbird in just such a hiding spot last fall. Located in the middle of a nearby cut cornfield, this bird's haven was no larger than the average living room. Wet ground prompted a dozen or so stringy cattails to grow up among the stubble; below, a light layer of foxtail filled in the gaps between the stalks. Each time I hunted that particular farm, I'd told myself the same thing: "There just has to be a cockbird in that patch." Each time, I'd been wrong.

I'd walked the waterway below the cornfield patch that morning, coming up with one nice rooster for my efforts. On my way out, I'd almost walked right by the patch, figuring that if it hadn't happened yet, maybe it was never going to. However, stubbornness won out, and I settled on a quick walk-through before heading for home. The flush, when it did come, surprised me. Head down and not paying much attention, I'd almost stepped on the tight-sitting rooster. At the bark of my over-under, the cornfield patch cockbird crumpled and spun into the stalks. No whitetail fanatic tagging a wide-racked ten-pointer was ever happier.

Step Three: Scouting

Years ago, an old man told a group of young pheasant hunters a simple rule: "The more you treat an old rooster like you would a big whitetail buck, the more birds you're going to bring home." Fortunately, I was one of those young hunters, and today his words still ring as true as they did when he said them twenty-five years ago.

Successful pheasant hunting during the early season doesn't start at 8 A.M. on opening day. Many hunters erroneously believe that there's no need to scout for pheasants like one would for whitetails or wild turkey gobblers. There is much to be learned—and done—in the days prior to the pheasant opener.

Two important variables to consider when scouting are weather and crop status. When the weather is slated to be warm and sunny, pheasants typically seek lighter cover, for example a see-through fenceline or a half-dozen steps' worth of knee-high foxtail that the farmer couldn't reach at the corner of the fence. Both offer the protection that roosters want, as well as comfort during the warmer days common in the early part of the season. And places like these are forgotten places that attract little if any attention from hunters. Rain, on the other hand, often pushes birds deeper into cover where they can escape the weather. This rainy-day cover often takes the form of overhead shelter, such as plum thickets or small groups of cedars. Gamebirds don't like getting their feathers wet and go to great lengths to avoid it. This means that heavier stands of foxtail and similar cover, although fantastic pheasant producers when dry, are often devoid of birds during and just after a good downpour. Instead hunters will want to concentrate on the overhead cover or fringe areas near such cover. Roosters, on edge because of the open floor in coverts such as plum thickets or cedars, often make a beeline for the first substantial hiding place nearby—even a small one—when they feel threatened. If you slowly work such overhead cover first, you will often find the birds haven't traveled far.

Crop status is another vital consideration. Standing corn and other row crops such as soybeans provide excellent habitat for early-season roosters; however, most crops, even if huntable with permission from the farmer, are difficult to hunt successfully. So does this mean that if the corn's still standing, you should stay home? Certainly not, but an adjustment might be necessary.

Tiny pockets, such as fence corners, thin fencelines, or recently mown waterways in and around standing corn, can be tremendously productive early in the morning. Birds roost in these types of coverts rather than in the standing, weed-free corn where predators such as foxes and raccoons can have easy access to them. The enterprising hunter should work these areas as soon as legally possible in the morning, hoping to catch birds before they've left the roost in search of the morning's meal. Rain can actually be beneficial to the

The type of cover you hunt depends in part on the weather at the moment.

A little bit of homework done prior to the season opener might make this "sea" of cover somewhat more manageable.

hunter focusing on these types of haunts. Wet weather typically causes pheasants to linger on the roost, thus extending the time the hunter has to capitalize on this early-morning style of hunting. Rain, too, can work in conjunction with standing corn by creating the scenario with overhead cover and a nearby hiding place scenario mentioned earlier. Under such inclement conditions, persistence—and decent raingear—can make all the difference in the world.

Much of the pheasant scouting that my wife and I do as part of our preparation for fall begins back in the spring. During turkey season, we make records of the farms where we've heard good numbers of roosters cackling. We make rough maps of the farms and pinpoint those locations where we heard the majority of roosters. We take this mapping process a step further in two phases. First, we walk the properties about two weeks before the upland opener, which allows us to see firsthand what we'll be walking into once the season

arrives. Second, we ask the landowners questions concerning the status of their crops just before opening day. We also ask about the pheasants. Where are they seen most mornings? Do they have a favored roosting area? Are there any smaller patches of cover that most hunters would find insignificant? And finally, we ask about other hunters. Will other groups be working the same property opening morning?

You can use all of this information you gain by scouting to your advantage when it comes time to plan your hunt. Hunters plan strategies for deer and elk, so why not pheasants? There is no better way to be successful than to combine all the information you accumulated while scouting—weather, crop status, scouting, and anticipated hunting pressure—into a working strategy.

Say the farm you plan to hunt on opening morning will also be visited by a group of five other hunters who have been coming there on opening morning for

the past ten years. The landowner just can't tell them no, but because you've asked permission for yourself alone, he has also granted you the right to walk the place that same morning. Through your conversation, you discover that the other hunters traditionally park their rigs on the gravel road to the south and work through two thirty-acre fields of Conservation Reserve Program (CRP) grass before finishing with a short drive through a narrow swath of corn that takes them back to their vehicles. You know from your scouting that there is a thin-cover fenceline on the eastern edge of property from which branch two separate small fingers of light foxtail ending in tiny stands of young willows. The fence and the fingers are about 150 yards from the eastern side of the corn through which the other group will hunt, and separated by foot-high soybeans.

You arrive on opening morning to see three trucks parked on the south gravel road. Judging from the orange line, the group has worked the first field and is halfway through the second. Within half an hour, the drivers have become glimpses of orange through the standing corn. Another half hour and two cups of coffee later, you hear the slamming of doors and tires spinning in the gravel as the group speeds away to the next farm.

Quietly you load up and slip into the southeast corner of the fenceline. You go only fifty yards before the first hen explodes from the short grass. Another fifteen and a rooster erupts from the same thin cover. It's an easy shot and a simpler retrieve. Fifty yards from the first finger, you slip into the edge of the beans and quietly make your way in a semicircle to the patch of willows. Halfway back to the fenceline, two cockbirds burst cackling from the foxtail. Flustered, you miss the one on the left, but the bird on the right flies squarely into an ounce of No. 6 shot. Back at the fenceline, you watch as two more roosters and three hens beat a hasty retreat back into the standing corn from the end of the second finger some seventy yards away. Smiling, you break the old double open and head back to the rig with yet another excellent opening day under your belt.

In this scenario, it's not difficult to see what happened. In the excitement that is opening day, the group of hunters had forgotten one of the cardinal rules of

Facing page: Take your time. Pheasant hunting shouldn't be a race. Besides, Old Mister Rooster will always come out first in a footrace.

pheasant hunting: Be quiet. Shortly after the first truck door slammed, many of the birds roosting in the two set-aside fields began to slip into the standing corn. Three white-spurred young roosters stayed in the fields with several hens, and these went into the hunting coats of two of the five guys. By the time the drive through the corn had ended, most of the birds had filtered back into the set-aside. A good number, however, had run, heads low, through the soybeans to take refuge in the two small fingers and the fenceline. The rest, as evidenced by the fine meal of grilled pheasant breast you and your family enjoyed that evening, goes without saying.

You don't have to be a rocket scientist to be a successful pheasant hunter. Nor does it require an orange-clad horde in battalion strength or canines capable of not only finding roosters, but plucking and preparing the birds for table. What it does take is a rethinking of the *big fields and big groups* philosophy, some scouting, and a little bit of ingenuity when it comes time to plan and strategize. Oh, and some skill behind a shotgun. Forgotten-cover cockbirds may have their weaknesses, but flying isn't one of them.

PHEASANT HUNTING SAFETY

"For all the pheasants ever bred won't repay for one man dead."

I wish I could give credit where credit is due, but I can't for the life of me remember where I first read these words. What I do remember is that the lines of the poem praised the ring-necked pheasant and listed the challenges and frustrations that he presents. Most of all, however, the rhyme reminded the reader of the importance of always being careful, always knowing where the other guy is, and being constantly on guard. The message was elemental.

Safety—I simply can't stress enough its importance for hunters. A fellow Iowa hunter, Joe Peska, reminds me of this every time we take his son, Tanner, afield. "What's the most important thing about hunting?" the elder Peska asks his boy as the hunt begins. Tanner always immediately replies, "Safety." Tanner usually adds, "And having fun," which is a very good thing to hear. Their back-and-forth banter serves as a reminder about the safety aspects involved in the shooting and hunting sports.

Any chapter on hunting techniques is incomplete without a discussion of hunting safety. Your list of

Above: Safety to start and safety to finish. The bottom line?
It's all about safety and common sense.
Right: Duck-calling champ Buck Gardner tangles with a
South Dakota rooster, with nothing to hit but air and
the Missouri River. Oh, yeah—the cockbird lost.

points may be a bit different. No exclusions, I wouldn't think, but perhaps you have a few more that I haven't listed here. That's a good thing.

Gun Safety

Firearms safety, or as some would call it, safe gun-handling skills, is paramount to hunters. Whether you're after roosters or rams, mallards or Malaysian unicorns, the principles don't change.

Treat every firearm as though it were loaded. Never point the muzzle at anything you don't want to shoot. Alcohol and firearms don't mix. Make sure of your target. Know where your hunting partners are. The safety is a mechanical feature that can, and sometimes does, fail. A 20-gauge shotshell dropped inside a 12-gauge chamber can be a very bad thing if not discovered before the next 12-gauge round is loaded and fired. Likewise, crawling over a barbed-wire fence with loaded shotgun in hand is dangerous.

Firearms safety, like obeying speed limits and not using mind-altering drugs, is primarily a function of common sense. Be aware of what's going on around you. Think safety and think safely. And if in doubt, don't shoot. There will always be another rooster.

Blaze Orange

Writing and hunting colleague Phil Bourjaily perhaps said it best in an article he wrote a couple years back. In a section titled "Don't Overdress," Bourjaily referred to himself as a *Chernobyl Pumpkin* in his manner of dress for the field. Trust me, he's not exaggerating. Judging from the blaze orange measured in square inches that Bourjaily wears while pheasant hunting, I'm sure he can be seen from space . . . with the naked eye.

I'm not poking fun at my good friend Phil. In fact, I too dress like a psychedelic jack-o-lantern whenever I'm pheasant hunting. Blaze orange lets me be seen,

and that's exactly what I want when a rooster flushes between my hunting partner and me and flies back behind us. I can't tell you how many times I've been in the midst of a flush when that flash of blaze orange caught my eye. And at that point, my brain screams "DON'T," and I don't even reach for the trigger. Nine times out of ten, the shot would have been safe; however, there's just something about that color that disconnects the nerve impulses running to my right index finger.

Wearing blaze orange when venturing into the field is a good idea, and I'll take that statement a

Above: Los Angeles' Guillermo Gastelo looks quite fashionable in his black hooded sweatshirt, orange vest, and matching ball hat. The key? Orange. Right: Even if not required by law, wearing blaze orange afield is a damn good idea.

step further by saying not only in the form of a blaze orange vest, but especially a blaze orange cap or head cover of some kind. Think about it: The cover's high, maybe late-season cattails or switchgrass. Or maybe the roll of the land puts your partner three to five feet below your horizontal line of sight. In these instances, a vest can't be seen, but a blaze orange cap perched atop your buddy's head can. You don't need a camouflage ball cap or toque to hunt pheasants as you do for waterfowl, turkeys, or deer. Wearing a camouflaged hat while hunting roosters is nothing more than a fashion statement—and I want a safety feature, *not* a fashion statement.

The Other Hunter's Dog

Twice now, I've witnessed a man's bird dog damn near get shot. The first time a hunter's (and I'll use the term loosely) over/under discharged below waist level while he was closing it before the hunt began. A young black Lab wasn't far from where the 1¼-ounce charge of No. 5 shot punched a fist-size hole through the goldenrod. The culprit was a case of "Safety OFF" syn-

drome. The Lab's owner—a close friend—somehow managed to hold both his tongue and his fists.

The second time came as Julie and I, along with a young friend, were walking the edges of a deep-sided, brushy creek. A rooster jumped unexpectedly, as they're prone to do, with Maggie, my black Lab, right on his tail feathers . . . as, back in her younger days, she was prone to do. The explosion of the 12-gauge to my right drowned out my shouts of "NO!" Fortunately for everyone involved, the shot charge—at that range about the size of a golf ball—missed everything including, I think, the Earth on the opposite side. Even now, several years later, the possibilities still make me feel sick to my stomach. I had a real heart-to-heart discussion with the young man, a semiexperienced hunter, about hunting over someone else's dog. Believe me, he learned a lot that morning.

The first incident was a case of safety and stupidity. The second shot was a combination of carelessness and inexperience. The young man, now a much more accomplished and careful hunter, simply hadn't spent any time hunting roosters behind dogs. Today, a por-

Always, always, always be cognizant of the dogs, whether they're yours, your hunting partner's, or otherwise.

tion of my "Safety Talk" prior to any hunt I'm spearheading consists of the following:

"Don't shoot me and don't shoot my dogs. These dogs work extraordinarily hard for little more than an oatmeal pie and some lovin'. My dogs are on the ground. Pheasants, at least those you will be shooting at, will be in the air. As for cripples, my dogs will get them. You will not shoot at a pheasant on or near the ground. If my dog doesn't get the cripple, it's my fault."

Am I trying to sound like a hard-ass here? No, but I am trying get my point across—do not shoot near my dogs and don't shoot near any hunter's dogs. If he doesn't want you to shoot rabbits while you're gunning over his dog, then don't shoot rabbits. If he asks that you shoot only those birds that his dog has pointed, then do that. If he coldcocks you and leaves you staring at the clouds in a patch of foxtail because you

punched a 12-gauge-size hole even in the general proximity of his Lab or Irish setter or wirehaired pointer . . . well, pardner, don't say I didn't warn you.

Runners and Low Fliers

Yeah, I know what I said to start this section: *If he's going to run like a rabbit . . .* Today most hunters consider it unsporting to shoot a rooster pheasant on the ground. Unethical, they call it, and I tend to agree. Though not illegal by statute, there's just something about swatting a cockbird while his scaly gray toes are still in contact with old Mother Earth. It's kind of like shooting a duck on the water. Nothing wrong legally there either, but you don't hear many guys bragging about the limit they water-swatted that morning.

But let's set ethics aside, and look at the safety issues involved with swinging on a running rooster. There are the dogs. Earlier I mentioned that while the dogs are on the ground and the rooster is in the air, there is no safety issue. However, put both cockbird and canine on the ground and you have the setting for a potential problem. Is this any less safe than shooting a rabbit in front of a beagle's nose? Most beaglemen will tell you that they don't shoot rabbits on the jump for this very reason. "Dog's right there," the man'll say. "You don't shoot 'em on the jump. Too dangerous for the dog."

Have I ever shot a rooster on the ground? Yes, not healthy birds, but once or twice a season I'll shoot a running cripple on the ground. Does it make me nervous? Somewhat, but in my own defense, every situation is different. If I think that Maggie or Jet is going to catch that rooster, I'll never touch the safety. If, however, I know exactly where my dogs are *and* I have a safe, dog-free shot at a crippled runner that I believe might escape, then I'll swat him on the ground. Or maybe I won't, opting instead to let my black Labs do the job.

Low fliers are another concern. From time to time, a rooster will flush vertically to about four feet and then skim off, brushing the tops of the goldenrod. You know, like a knot of blue-wing teal twisting and swirling over the cattails on your favorite marsh . . . except without all the aerobatics and at speeds much less than a blue-wing's MACH 1 or MACH 2. In these situations where the birds are low, you need to know where people are. Where are your hunting partners? Are there other hunters in the area? What's straight away and on the level? Over the years, I've heard several pheasant guides tell hunters during their pre-hunt speech never to shoot at any birds at less than a forty-five-degree angle and if they shot at a bird at less than a forty-five-degree angle to the ground, they were going back to the truck. No questions asked. It's not a "who's the boss" type of situation, but rather one of safety. Birds in the air, between forty-five and ninety degrees above the ground, typically mean folks on the ground are safe from being shot. Shooting at birds lower than forty-five degrees can put those hunters on the ground at risk.

Blockers and Drivers

Let's look at the forty-five-degree angle rule and its application in walking and blocking. As you read earlier, the walking-and-blocking strategy involves a line of armed people stomping through cover toward any

Roosters and Weather

It would be nice if every day during pheasant season dawned a bit chilly, with all the standing corn down and—why not, it's my fantasy—a couple inches of new snow on the ground. The wind wouldn't blow, the sky would be a soft blue, and every rooster—and there'd be dozens of them—would quarter away from left to right in front of Jet's point or Deacon's nose. Ah, yes. That would be nice indeed.

But no place can be like this every day, and in some places, such as western Washington in November and eastern Iowa in December, these days occur damn infrequently. What do we pheasant hunters do, then, when the temperature is close to zero or the north winds howl or the snow is knee-deep? Our options, truthfully, are two: stay home or improvise, adapt, and make the most of the situation. Me? I'm inclined to follow number two. I do, however, let the weather dictate both where *and* how I'm going to hunt.

Okay, so I'll start off with an exception. Given a hard, driving rain, I'll stay home and wait till it blows through. Hell, I won't even hunt ducks in a hard, driving rain these days. Why? Because the ducks, like the pheasants, are smarter than I am and won't be out wandering around where I can get to them in that sort of weather. A light rain, though, and I'm out the door. In wet conditions, I hunt thin cover—my thinking being that pheasants don't like to get wet, but if getting wet is unavoidable, they don't want to get any wetter than necessary. Heavy cover in the rain gets pheasants wet; thin cover keeps this to a minimum, and the birds know it. Ideally, I have permission to hunt a patch of light cover with overhead protection—a small stand of hedge (Osage orange) and hawthorne trees sprinkled with light grasses and here-and-there briar patches not far from my house comes immediately to mind. It has afforded more than one rainy-day rooster to my black dogs and me.

Some guys hate snow; I love it when it comes to pheasant hunting. The first snow of the year, I adjust my schedule to include nothing but hunting. Confronted with their first dusting of the white stuff, young-of-the-year roosters are confused and will often do things such as sit tight, and not run wild that they otherwise wouldn't do. In heavy snow, especially if it's been around awhile, I hunt heavier cover such as switchgrass or cattails, preferably adjacent or very close to a good food source, which here in Iowa means corn. If it's also a bright sunny day, I try to find a rough-cut (high-stubble) cornfield. If I can find one, that's where I'm starting, as it's likely the birds are soaking up the sun while putting on the high protein feedbag *and* feeling relatively secure in the shadows of the stubble. I have to step lightly and be sneaky here, though, as the birds can see a long way and aren't likely to let me walk right up beside them and toss them in my pouch.

Wind is tough. It makes me grouchy, my Labs squirrelly, and a pheasant as wild as anything the good Lord ever created. The birds, if yours are anything like mine, are going to flush long or, worse, run and never stop. That said, any smaller blocks of cover that a couple of partners and I can work in a drive-and-post fashion are my first choice in the wind. If it's just me and a dog, I try my best to keep him close and concentrate on smaller blocks of cover that are out of the wind. Avid pheasant chaser Kevin Michalowski, a former resident of South Dakota, advises folks to "look in the deepest, thickest stuff they can find on the leeward side" whenever the wind's blowing . . . and this is good advice.

Nice weather is just that—nice—but we can't always have mild temperatures and blue skies, now can we? SOUTH DAKOTA TOURISM

Tempting? Certainly, but runners and low fliers are off-limits . . .
and everyone needs to be on the same page there.

number of nonwalking individuals, the blockers, who also happen to be armed. Throw a bunch of wildly flushing roosters between the two groups, and you have all the makings of a most interesting experience.

"Blue sky," the outfitters will tell their people in these types of situations. "I want to see blue sky all the way around a bird before someone's shooting at it. That goes for both walkers and for blockers." And he's right. When two lines of hunters are converging on a specific point in space with wildly flushing roosters in the middle, it's very important that any shooting fall under the heading of elevated. You need to let those birds get up and get surrounded by that blue sky *before* you even think about touching the trigger. Add standing corn, switchgrass, or any other type of tall cover, and this rule becomes even more important. In sum-

mary, everyone wears a blaze orange cap and nobody shoots before the birds reach a forty-five-degree angle—it's easy as that.

Rooster's Revenge

I'm going to mention this topic because I've enjoyed the experience of which I'm about to speak. An old rooster's spurs are not there for decoration. They're not a visual aid nor are they meant to look cool. They're not there to break up an otherwise dull, drab gray leg. They are wickedly sharp and if you grab hold of one of these instruments, there's a good chance you're going to get cut. If the owner of said spurs is still alive while you're doing this grabbing, it's a pretty safe bet that you can put the word *badly* immediately after the word *cut*. Trust me on this one.

*Waiting at the end of the drive, knowing that no one—no one!
—will unload on a runner or a low-flying bird.*

CHAPTER 3

Guns and Ammo

ON OPENING DAY OF PHEASANT SEASON, you're damn near guaranteed to see almost anything afield, from the guy with a shotgun—and I use the term loosely—that's more duct tape than it is metal and wood and who has a copy of the current hunting and fishing regulations sticking out of the back pocket of his Levi's, to the dandy with a robotic dog and a $3,000 over/under wearing enough oilcloth (recently waxed, of course) to stock any C. C. Filson store. Better, my wife comments as we keep our black Lab, Maggie, at heel and watch, than any parade we'd ever been to—minus the free candy, of course.

Check out any South Dakota pheasant push, look at any group of Thanksgiving Day Iowa rooster chasers, or visit your friendly neighborhood shooting preserve around mid-October, and you'll see are lots and lots and lots of different shotguns. Big ones and little ones. Expensive ones, and those, like Mister Duct Tape's, that look more tire iron than they do shooting iron. Two barrels—horizontal or vertical configuration, you take your pick—or one barrel. Hammers or hammerless. They're all out there and, in skilled hands, all capable of bringing even the wiliest rooster to ground. Or missing said rooster, whichever the case may be.

Like there is no *perfect* deer caliber and no *ultimate* waterfowl shotgun, there is no *Almighty* pheasant gun. There are, certainly, those firearms that, when operated

*Ah, my 16-gauge Winchester Model 24 double—as fine a pheasant gun
as you'll find anywhere . . . and I'm sticking to that.*

skillfully, are more capable than others under particular circumstances. But to throw a bit of confusion into the mix here, that's not to say that those less capable won't be more capable the day after tomorrow. What were fifty-yard flushes on Saturday suddenly become in-your-face explosions on Sunday, and the 3-inch blunderbuss filled with 2³/₄-inch shotshells filling damn near to overflowing with 1⁵/₈ ounces of No. 4s you brought to cope with those *w-i-d-e* roosters now seems a little excessive. So the best firearm for pheasant hunting is a shotgun that's capable of a variety of shots—fifty yards as well as twenty-five. Capable of what? The birds will tell you and then it becomes a matter of personal proficiency . . . but we'll get to that in a bit.

There must be a voice inside the American male that tells us bigger is better. Super Size those fries, please, and throw a couple hot apple pies on that tray, will ya? Well, I'm here to tell you that in terms of pheasants and shotguns and ammunition and chokes and a long list of other variables, bigger isn't always better. Nor is it always necessary. Through the seasons, I've seen roosters brought to ground quite nicely with everything from a single-shot Harrington & Richardson .410 with its ¹¹/₁₆ ounce of No. 6 shot to a war-wagon Ithaca Mag-10, but that doesn't mean that either one is the ultimate pheasant gun.

THE ULTIMATE PHEASANT GUN

What type of fowling piece should one use for pheasants? For insight, I turned to a man whom I consider the consummate pheasant hunter, native Iowan and outdoor writer Phil Bourjaily. What I asked Bourjaily was simple: If you could design the *Ultimate Pheasant Gun,* what might that firearm be? What would it look like? How would it handle? His answers were interesting:

Gauge: "Twelve. I like it, among other reasons, because you have the widest range of ammunition choices. I like the 1¹/₄-ounce lead loads; however, if you're in an area where nontoxic shot is required—and that's happening more and more these days—then you use 1¹/₄ ounce of steel No. 2s out of a 3-inch 12 gauge just fine."

It's interesting to note that Bourjaily stutter-stepped with his opening comments. "It might be a 16-gauge," he said, apologizing for hedging already. "The 16 is so close ballistically and loadwise to the 12 and it's a nice, light little gun. If nontoxics are a concern, you can always shoot Kent's Impact tungsten-matrix in the 16-gauge. But let's stick with the 12."

Chamber: "2³/₄- or 3-inch. I want to ability to shoot the 3-inch if I'm somewhere where I have to shoot steel."

Action: "Over/under. No reason other than that's what I shoot."

Barrel length: "Twenty-eight. I'm always surprised when I shoot a 26-inch barrel well, but I still like the 28. I like the way it looks, and I like that little extra

My wife, Julie, with a Browning Citori 20-gauge over/under. In the case of pheasant guns, bigger isn't always better.

As pretty a selection of upland pieces as you're going to see.
And yes, even the single .410.

weight out there. It helps with my follow-through. I just shoot better with a little longer barrel."

Chokes: "Improved and Modified, and steel friendly. Oh, and long choke tubes, with a long taper. Most of my shooting happens within twenty-five yards; if I miss, then within thirty-five yards. Improved and Modified will more than handle this. Now realize that all pheasant hunting isn't the same. The poster in South Dakota might want a tighter choke, but for the way I hunt here in Iowa—slowly, with one or two people—Improved and Modified works fine."

Weight: "Less than seven pounds, but more than six."

Trigger: "I'm easily confused, so I want one trigger. And I want a mechanical trigger in which both hammers are cocked when the gun is opened as opposed to an inertia trigger that relies on the gun's recoil to cock and ready the second hammer. Every two or three years, I'll have this happen: I shoot one rooster, open the gun, and a second rooster jumps before I can reload. With a mechanical trigger, I

close the gun, it goes click and *BANG!* With an inertia trigger, the gun goes click . . . and click. It drives me nuts. I want a trigger pull in the 3$^{1}/_{2}$-pound range. I don't mash a trigger now, but I'm planning on being more subtle in the future."

Safety: "I really don't care whether I have an automatic or manual safety. My first over/under had an automatic safety, so I'm used to those. People who aren't used to an auto safety . . . well, it drives them nuts."

Bead: "A single bead. No midrib bead. I don't see the bead anyway. If you're looking at the bead, you're going to miss. Midrib beads are great if you're lining up on a gobbler or getting ready to call for a bird in trap, but other than that, I don't like them."

Ejectors versus extractors: "Ejectors, but I still catch all my empties. I don't want to be littering up the landscape with my empties." [Note: Ejectors actually *pop* the empty hulls out of the breech; extractors simply raise or extend them so as to make them easier to manually pull out. Also, Bourjaily does catch *all* his empties; I've watched him.]

Stock, forearm, and receiver: "A straight grip and a thin forearm, plus a low-profile receiver like the Berettas have. Walnut wood, with swirls and figures. And a case-hardened receiver with engraving just like the Stevens Model 411 with an English setter flushing the duck. While we're at it, I'll have the gun custom fitted, too."

Finish: "An oil finish so the scratches don't show. Not one of those plastic finishes."

Recoil pad: "A thin, hard rubber recoil pad. Not so much for the recoil, but so it doesn't slip and fall when I lean it up against something. I don't want that engraving scratched."

And how did this shooter summarize his recipe for his *Ultimate Pheasant Gun?* Three simple words: "Oozes good taste." So you shoot well and look good doing it. What more can you ask for?

So now with Bourjaily's creation settled nicely in our brains, let's take an in-depth look at some of the specifics he mentioned, beginning with the size of the hole at the muzzle end. Or, more precisely, does gauge matter when it comes to roosters?

Recoil pads, like many aspects of the "ultimate pheasant gun," are an individual decision.

Left: Lee Harstad of Pierre, South Dakota, opts for a Remington 870 in 12-gauge.
Above: I'm partial to the 16-bore, bastard gauge and all.

PHEASANT GUN GAUGES

12-Gauge: Though I have no evidence other than personal observation, I feel safe in saying that seven or eight out of every ten shotguns you see in the field during pheasant season are going to be 12-gauges. It's just that way. One reason might be that a lot of folks, myself included, have what we'll call a *double-duty shotgun*; that is, the same piece they carry into the duck swamp or goose pit will then pull double duty once pheasant season rolls around. And there's good reason for the 12-gauge gun's popularity. The 12 offers a wide array of both lead and nontoxic loads. It also comes in a tremendous variety of shapes, sizes, configurations, and perhaps best of all, price ranges. Last but not least, it's proved itself time and time again a more-than-capable killer of pheasants—that is, should the individual behind the buttplate be similarly as capable.

16-Gauge: I love the 16-gauge, having grown up with two: a 1952 Winchester Model 24 and a 1979 Remington Model 1100. And I absolutely *h-a-t-e* when I hear them referred to as "that bastard gauge," although I admit that the 3-inch 20-gauge and the lighter 12-gauge loads certainly have done a number on the poor 16. Still, the little gun that hits like a 12-gauge but carries like a 20 nonetheless has earned itself a spot

in the uplands. With its 1-ounce standard loading and $1^{1}/_{4}$-ounce magnum, the 16-gauge can certainly handle itself. Are nontoxics mandatory on your pheasant ground? Not a problem, thanks to offerings from both Kent Cartridge and the Bismuth Cartridge Company. What's more, these nontox loads are compatible with my older side-by-side, as they would be with a Model 12 or Model 21. So to those of you who have retired those "old" 16-gauge guns . . . bring 'em out.

20-Gauge: It took but one season shooting a Browning Citori Lightning Feather 20-gauge for roosters before I both fell in love with the little gun *and* realized that the man shooting the 20-gauge for pheasants is definitely not at a shotgunning disadvantage. If you're giving a 20 some serious thought, however, I'd suggest this: Get one that handles both $2^{3}/_{4}$- and 3-inch shotshells. Those $1^{1}/_{4}$, 3-inch 20-gauge shotshells will put you right there in the middle with the big boys shooting the 12s and the heavy 16s, regardless of whether the game's lead or nontoxic.

28-Gauge: I must admit that I have virtually no experience with the 28-gauge; however, Phil Bourjaily has, and though he claims that the gun is "getting a little light for pheasants," he also says that he has killed wild roosters with the 28, shooting the gun's standard

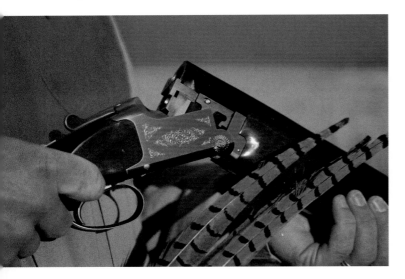

Above: A Browning Citori Lightning Feather in 20-gauge, one of the nicest little shotguns I've ever carried afield. Right: Nebraska's Rick Windham with a Winchester Model 9410, a lever action .410, and in his talented hands a deadly pheasant piece.

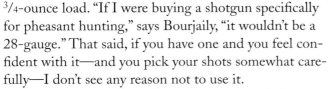

$3/4$-ounce load. "If I were buying a shotgun specifically for pheasant hunting," says Bourjaily, "it wouldn't be a 28-gauge." That said, if you have one and you feel confident with it—and you pick your shots somewhat carefully—I don't see any reason not to use it.

.410 caliber: With its $11/16$-ounce standard charge, the .410 caliber makes for a poor choice in the pheasant fields. Squirrels at, say, twenty-five yards perhaps, but not pheasants. Certainly, there are those accomplished shooters who, armed with a Browning .410 over/under, can make every 12-gauge gunner they encounter look ballistically challenged; however, those folks, though wonderful to watch, are without question in the minority. The .410, sad to say, just doesn't carry enough shot or pattern well enough to be called a good choice for the pheasant hunter.

Blackpowder: Bourjaily mocks me when I speak of hunting roosters with my Italian Pedersoli Gardoni 12-gauge side-by-side muzzleloading shotgun, but I care not. Several years ago, I was introduced to gunning the uplands frontier-style, and while, no, it's not for everyone, I do enjoy hunting birds through a cloud of thick, stinky, white smoke. This particular percussion piece is fixed-choked tight modified and very tight full, and it patterns well with 80 grains of GOEX black powder

under a Remington Power Piston shot cup filled with $1^{1}/_{4}$ ounce of No. 5 chilled lead shot. Let's just say that if I miss a going-away rooster, it's not the gun's fault! Cabela's makes a beautiful little twin tube in both 12- and 20-gauge models, and has all the accessories you'd ever need to get one up and running. And as far as Bourjaily's concerned—just ignore him; I do.

PHEASANT SHOTGUN ACTIONS

More than gauge, the type of action by which one's pheasant piece operates is a matter of personal preference. Some hunters would never think of shooting anything *but* a side-by-side, while those on the other side of the fence have devoted the whole of their pheasant-hunting existence to an over/under. But the truth is, you'll see them all out there, each type of action with its own personalities, quirks, advantages, and disadvantages.

Single-shot: During my formative outdoor years, I killed a lot of game with a single-shot shotgun—rabbits, squirrels, ducks, geese, deer, grouse, bobwhite quail—but, perhaps surprisingly, never a pheasant. But this was Ohio in the late 1970s, and there just weren't many wild roosters to be found; still, you would have thought I'd have bagged at least one. That all said, I'm

Left: Probably half of the pheasant guns seen afield will be over/unders—they're that popular.
Below: Good friend and tremendous shooter L. P. Brezny with a pet side-by-side in South Dakota.

sure there have been countless roosters killed by Iowa farm boys armed with old Stevens single-shots and pockets full of Super-X No. 4 "duck shells." Today, with the exception of those parents introducing their little ones to hunting courtesy of a hand-me-down single tube—unfortunately, there are far too few of those—you seldom see a single-shot in the uplands. That's just the way it is.

Side-by-side: Whenever I think pheasants and tradition, I think side-by-side. Whether it's the late Bill Custer's L. C. Smith 16-gauge, my Model 24, or any of a thousand other horizontal tube guns—Fox, Parker, Merkel, Winchester, AYA, et al—out in the field today, there's just something about a side-by-side that screams pheasant! Or grouse. Or maybe woodcock. But definitely pheasant.

Over/under (O/U): Although I've been shooting O/Us for only the past couple of seasons, I'm quite smitten with the guns. For the most part, they're light,

quick, and very easy on the eyes. Some aren't so kind to your pocketbook, but with quality, good looks, and performance comes—yes—price. You wouldn't expect to drop a C-note on a 1939 Rolls Royce, now would you? Still, there are O/Us out there that won't break the bank. I've found Mossberg's new Silver Reserve, a not unattractive piece that to date shoots quite well for me, for as low as $299—not a bad deal when you consider that the fuel I used to get to me to the local shooting supply house cost me $2.25/gallon.

Pump gun: This is the working man's gun, the Average Joe's gun, the cornshucker. Whatever you call it, one thing stands true about the pump action: It's as damn reliable as they come—and popular. There was a time when I would have felt safe in saying that a majority of the pheasants killed across the country over the course of any given season fell to a man shooting a Remington 870 Wingmaster. Today that might not be the case, but I feel confident saying that there are a ton

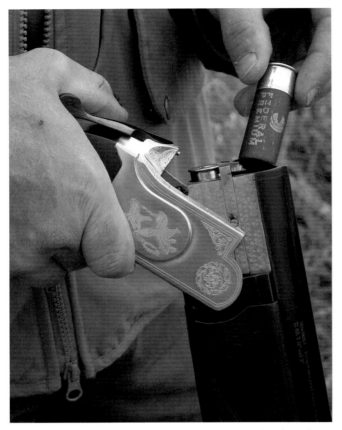

I like an over/under—that is, when I'm not shooting the 16-gauge side-by-side. It's all about what you're used to and what you shoot well.

The Darth Vader gun, a Benelli Nova pump, complete with an electronic collar transmitter holder—a neat idea.

of pump guns out there, their owners giving chase to roosters east and west. Mossberg 500s, Ithaca Model 37s, the venerable Model 12, and the aforementioned M870—they're all there, and they're doing a fine job.

Autoloader: More and more, autoloaders are finding their way into the uplands. I'm not sure exactly why, although I certainly can't argue with the assertion that a Belgian A-5 Sweet Sixteen is about as traditional a piece as you might find and certainly does deserve a nostalgic post in the field. Perhaps it has to do with many Americans' fascination with the concept known simply as "the most cartridges allowed by law." Maybe it goes back to what I mentioned earlier about the 12-gauge being a double-duty gun. Substitute *autoloader* for *12-gauge,* and we might be onto something here. Or maybe a hunter just prefers a semiautomatic, like he chooses Johnny Walker Red over Gentleman Jack. "But aren't autoloaders heavy?" someone asks. "They're fine shoved into the corner of a duck blind, but do you want to carry one all day?" True, some autoloaders are quite

heavy, but then again, so are some O/Us and pump guns. Conversely, there are some lightweight semiautos that are quite capable pheasant guns—Remington's Light 20 or the 6.5-pound Beretta Urika AL391 12-gauge, to name but two. What's it all boil down to? Two words: personal and preference, because it's true . . . $1^{1}/_{2}$ ounces of copper-plated No. 4s out of a single shot will kill a rooster just as dead as if they had come out of a $2,000 autoloader. But you gotta hit it first.

BARRELS AND CHOKES

I realize that it's out of character, but I'm not going to spend much time on the subject of barrels and chokes. Why not? Because I feel that both choices are simultaneously personal and rather elemental. To explain:

Phil Bourjaily prefers 28-inch barrels, claiming that they look better and the extra weight assists in his follow-through. I, on the other hand, like 26-inch barrels because they're lighter and, as an instinctive shooter, I don't concern myself with follow-through.

Does follow-through matter? Yes. Do I do it? I must, at least whenever what I'm shooting at falls or breaks into pieces.

My point is this. I pick 26 and Phil picks 28. Grandpa's Stevens side-by-side had 30-inch barrels, which were no disadvantage to him, and I know of several gentlemen who shoot their 24-inch turkey guns, with the Extra-Full tubes swapped out for Modifieds, during pheasant season. Does size really matter here? Probably not. What does matter is that you've taken the time to pattern your fowling piece prior to the opener, and you've spent a little time shooting trap, skeet, sporting clays, or Blue Rocks heaved out of a hand thrower down at the local quarry pond. Let's face it—it's not the size of the barrels that matter, it's what you do with them. Sorry, Dr. Freud.

On the subject of chokes, I'll be a little more definite. Phil Bourjaily shoots Improved and Modified in his O/Us. I plug the traditional Modified and Full tubes into my O/Us, and my fixed-choke side-by-side are similarly choked Modified and Full. In a single barrel, both Bourjaily and I opt for Modified as a middle-of-the-road, somewhat forgiving constriction that allows us to handle—if we're up on our game that day—25-yard rises as well as 40-yard flushes.

Some gunners would have nothing *but* an Improved cylinder. They shoot their birds close over pointing dogs, or they shoot some of the modern, tight-patterning nontoxics such as Hevi-Shot or Kent's Impact tungsten-matrix. Or both. And this is fine, as long as they understand their limitations, which most do. To switch gears, ask the habitual blocker in South Dakota his choke of choice, and he's likely to say full. "Screw it down as tight as you can, boy," he'll tell you. "Them shots, they're gonna be long." And on any given day, he very well might have a good point. The truth is, you and I both have had roosters jump within Cylinder Bore range, and we've seen those that you couldn't reach with an 88-millimeter artillery piece. The question is, how do you hunt? Where, or rather, how far typically from the gun are your birds? Then decide on a choke.

TALKING AMMUNITION

Let's face it: Cheap, low-quality shotshells will kill pheasants. More expensive, high-quality ammunition won't always connect or, worse, will cripple birds that you never find. So now, with this in mind, how do you choose a pheasant load?

First, let's look at the shotshells as a whole and answer a couple of questions. If you choose to shoot either a 3-inch 12-gauge or a 3-inch 20, are 3-inch shotshells necessary? In the case of the 12, I'd say no—that is, unless you're shooting steel where nontoxics are required by mandate. Here, you want as much capacity as you can get, all of it packed with as many of those light steel spheres as possible. Saying this, am I implying that 2¾-inch steel 12-gauge loads are worthless for pheasants? No, not entirely, but given my druthers *and* an all-steel ruling, I'll fill my fowling piece with 1¼-ounce 3-inch steel No. 3s. This is roughly equivalent to 1⅛ ounces of lead No. 5s, and this gives me a warm, fuzzy, nontoxic feeling.

As for the 3-inch 20-gauge, here I'd say yes, especially when shooting steel, but even when using lead. The most you're going to get out of the 20-gauge is 1¼ ounces; that's in the 3-inch format. In the standard 2¾-inch 20-gauge, you've dropped those shot charges to an ounce, or in some cases, ⅞ ounce, and that's simply not a lot of pellets, particularly adequately sized steel pellets, launched in a rooster's general direction. Here, despite what I said earlier, bigger probably is better.

Shot charges differ from hunter to hunter . . . to some extent. Smallbore aficionados with their 28s and 2¾-inch 20s will shoot ⅞-ounce and 1-ounce loads, respectively, and do quite well. Others—my old-school father, Mick, for instance—start out the season shooting 1½ ounces of copper No. 6s and finish the season shooting 1½ ounces of copper No. 6s. "Don't mess with what works," he'll tell you. And it works for him; that, and the truth is I couldn't get him to change even if I hid all his pheasant bullets. Most shooters, myself included, will fall somewhere between these lows and highs. But what is the most popular shot charge for pheasants? I'm going to say 1¼ ounces of No. 5 or No. 6 lead shot, and this based on what I see in the stores around opening day, what I read, what I see in the field, and perhaps most significantly, what I use afield.

But what about shot sizes? Here again, on any opening day in Iowa there's a good chance you'll encounter everything from No. 2s to No. 8s. Maybe you'll even see hand-rolled loads of No. 2s *and* No. 8s . . . who knows? But is there one shot size that works

Don't go overchoked. Modified or Improved Modified (IM) will work just fine in almost all field applications.

An ounce and one-eighth of No. 6 shot from this 1979 Remington Model 1100 16-gauge is plenty for even the nastiest cockbird.

better than the others? Different situations call for different solutions; however, here are some basic rules of thumb—for traditional lead shot, mind you.

No. 4: I think No. 4s are a bit of overkill when it comes to pheasants. Pellet count, too, becomes an issue when you starting looking at 135 pellets per ounce for No. 4 and 225 for No. 6. I won't argue, however, that there have been times when the Big Boy No. 4s have had their place: A windy South Dakota day when I've

been a poster and the best I'm getting is forty yards. Or an Iowa winter day when the birds are hoofing it and, again, forty yards is the best I'm going to do. There's no denying that No. 4s pack a punch, particularly on those bone-and-muscle going-away rises. Still, my call is that they're a bit big.

No. 5: The No. 5 is a great middle-of-the-road, all-season-long choice. Back in the day when I was cranking out shotshells with an MEC 600 Jr., everything—and I mean everything—was either $1^1/8$ or $1^1/4$ ounces of No. 5 shot. Energy retention, pellet count, pattern density—No. 5s have it all.

No. 6: As fine a choice as are No. 5s, I prefer No. 6 shot. There are 281 pellets in $1^1/4$ ounces of No. 6 shot, a fact that addresses both pellet count *and* pattern density. Copper or nickel plate those No. 6 pellets, and you have all the penetration capabilities you're ever going to need out to those distances where you really should be shooting at pheasants.

No. 7.5: Some would say that No. 7.5 shot is a mite small for pheasants; I disagree. Yes, I tend to shoot No. 6s about 95 percent of the time, but that's not because I don't believe No. 7.5 to be an effective and very justifiable choice, whether early, mid-, or late season. Doesn't matter. The pellet count for No. 7.5—437 for $1^1/4$ ounces—is absolutely tremendous, and it goes without saying, knowing this, that pattern density is likewise going to be excellent in most cases. As for energy, both initial and retained out to a distance? I could go into a lengthy dissertation on kinetic energy, distance, size, space, and the price of a loaf of white at the local grocery store . . . but I won't. I will say this: Yes, No. 7.5 (1.3 foot-pounds at forty yards) does pack less punch than No. 6 (2.3 foot-pounds, same distance); however, the chances are mathematically superb that you're going to hit that rooster with a dozen or more of those needlelike little pellets at forty yards, and that's a good thing. Bring the shot back to thirty yards, and the result is going to be as simple as *dead* and *pheasant.*

No. 8 and smaller: I don't go any smaller than No. 7.5 for pheasants. Sure, pellet count with No. 8s—513 for $1^1/4$ ounces—is ridiculously high, and the patterns look like swarms of little bees; however, those little bees don't pack much sting much beyond thirty yards. Combine that with wind, bone, muscle, feathers, and operator error, and you're just not giving yourself much chance. Crippling rates, too, stand a chance to rise, so unless you're willing—and able—to limit yourself to opportunities no greater than thirty yards distant, you're likely better off with slightly larger pellets.

NONTOXICS AND SPEED IN THE UPLANDS

More and more pheasant hunters these days are driving up to their usual parking lot at their favorite wildlife management area, only to be met with freshly

Improving Your Shooting Proficiency

WARNING: There is a cliché about to be presented . . . *You can't expect to not practice and get any better.* And it doesn't matter if you're a professional bowler, an Iron Chef, the owner of a sewage and septic sucking service, or a shotgunner. The bottom line is practice makes one more proficient. Perfect? Perhaps not, but more proficient? Usually.

The best shotgunners I know shoot year-round. My dear friend Phil Bourjaily is one of the better shooters I've met. Part of the reason is because he has a shotgun in his hands twelve months out of the year. Granted, it's a different gun every time we talk, but that's the price he pays as shooting editor, poor guy. When he's not hunting, he's shooting trap or skeet or sporting clays. Typically, his practice comes in a formal

Sporting clays, trap, skeet—practice doesn't have to be formal to be helpful . . . and shooting year-round certainly can help improve your success in the field.

form; however, he does spend a good amount of time with his son, Gordon, and Gordon's buddy Nathan at a local range behind a hand or foot trap, case of Blue Rock clay pigeons by their side. Regardless of where, when, or what, the common denominator in Bourjaily's case is this: He actually gets out and practices what he preaches, and in doing so, he's improved considerably as a shotgunner.

But can it work for you? Yes, practice can make anyone a better shooter. It has to be the right kind of practice, however, and there's really no better way to learn how to practice your shotgunning skills than with a series of formal shooting lessons. Recently, I've had the great pleasure of discussing shooting with a most interesting Texan by the name of Gil Ash. Gil and his wife, professional shooter/trainer Vicki Ash, operate the Optimum Shotgun Performance (OSP) Shooting School (www.ospschool.com, 800-838-7533) in Houston. Annually, the Ashes provide instruction to some two thousand students from around the world and have, since opening their school in 1995, seen an estimated 4.5 million shotshells fired at clay targets and gamebirds. That's a lot of bullets! Phil Bourjaily is a former student and can't speak highly enough of the Ashes and their teaching style.

"These shooting clinics are fun," says Bourjaily. "Taking lessons is just fun, as long as you don't let your ego get in the way. Gil uses a lot of humor and a lot of sarcasm—in a good-natured way—in his clinics, and he keeps it fun. You find yourself doing things that you really didn't think you could do, and that's neat, too. You have to go into these clinics with an open mind and be ready to admit that some of the things you thought were right aren't necessarily. If you do that, you'll get a lot of benefit out of the lesson."

Lessons are great, but it's vital to then practice what you've been taught. Ash advises his students to take what they've learned at OSP onto the trap range and practice a minimum of twice a week for at least three weeks following his instruction. Only through repetition can a shooter expect to improve.

"We've done some studies on shooting more often," says Ash, "and we found that the students who practice can retain more than 80 percent of what we taught them. Those people who don't retain only 25 to 40 percent. These people will retain what we teach them intellectually, but they can't apply it. You can't be thinking about swing mechanics when the bird's in the air. The swing mechanics have to be in the subconscious. Physical therapists and neurologists say that you have to do something twenty-five hundred to three thousand times—and correctly—before it's embedded in the subconscious. And instinctive shooting is nothing more than subconscious shooting."

Don't forget routine shotgun maintenance. After all, you can't fault something you haven't cleaned.

hung signs proclaiming the area off-limits to all but nontoxic shotshells. Shock? Surprise? Anger? Frustration? Confusion? All of the above?

Facts are facts. Lead is a toxic substance, whether the life form ingesting it is a redhead or a ringneck. It takes but a lead pellet or two eaten, ground, and absorbed into the bloodstream to be fatal. And then you have places such as the Muskrat Slough Wildlife Area in eastern Iowa. Since 1991, the marsh, like all of the United States, has been nontoxic only for waterfowl hunting; however, come a good freeze, pheasant hunters hit the now-frozen wetland, spraying hundreds of lead pellets across the same area that only weeks before was off-limits to the substance. Doesn't make much sense, now does it?

Bit by bit, state game agencies across the country are instituting a nontoxic public-land mandate. And the uplanders who wish to continue visiting these areas are having to make the change. But trust me, that's not

No. 5 shot, like that contained in this 12-gauge shotshell from Wolf Ammunition, is a great middle-of-the-road choice.

a bad thing, thanks in large part to the advancements made in nontoxic ammunition over the past decade. No, sir—this isn't *Steel, 1990* anymore. Pheasant hunters forced—or choosing—to use nontoxic shotshells actually now have a choice, and several good ones at that.

Steel: Steel shot and the hulls that hold it definitely have improved since the mid-1980s. Powders, wads, primers, and velocities all have changed, and few would argue that it hasn't been for the better.

Certainly, many of the improvements in steel ammunition have been made with the waterfowler in mind; however, perhaps as a side effect, ammunition manufacturers have developed a lengthy list of steel pheasant-capable options for the 12-, 16-, and 20-gauge shooter. In the case of steel, the old rule of thumb—two shot sizes larger in steel than with lead—still applies; that is, instead of the traditional lead No. 4, No. 5, or No. 6, it's steel No. 2, No. 3, and No. 4. Often, with the exception being the 2³/4-inch-only 16-gauge, this shot will be housed in a 3-inch hull, the reason being shot capacity.

Today the trend is toward high-velocity steel ammunition. "Old" is the standard 1,125 feet per second to 1,200 feet per second; "new" are loads in excess of 1,400 feet per second, with some lightning-fast offerings leaving the muzzle at 1,550 feet per second. With steel, light as it is in comparison with lead, speed is something to be strongly considered.

Kent Impact tungsten-matrix: A couple years back, I asked Linda Barnhart at Kent Cartridge if she would send me a box of Kent's Impact tungsten-matrix 16-gauge shotshells so that I might shoot them out of my 1952 Model 24. They arrived, I shot them at roosters and prairie grouse in Nebraska, and I can summarize the experience in one word: impressive.

The matrix here refers to a mix of powdered tungsten and select polymers (nylon) combined so as to approximate lead pellets in both density—93 percent as dense, to be exact—and effectiveness. What's more, not only does the mix perform like the lead pellets of old, but it's safe to use in even our oldest upland field pieces. And there's no confusion regarding shot-size conversion tables; No. 5 Impact equals No. 5 lead—simple as that.

Currently, Kent manufactures an Impact Pheasant & Game load for those shooting a 12-, 16-, or 20-

Nontoxic doesn't mean nonlethal; in fact, quite the opposite can be true with some of today's high-tech lead-free shotshells.

gauge, in shot charges ranging from a light 1-ounce load to a heavier 1¼-ounce offering in the 12-gauge.

Bismuth: I'm sure some will disagree, but I liken bismuth to Kent's tungsten-matrix in terms of performance and user-friendliness. Like Impact, this alchemist's brew of bismuth and tin, at 87 percent, damn near mirrors lead on the density scale. Too, bismuth offers a one-for-one shot-size comparison and is similarly kind to older guns. The only downside? Again, like the tungsten-matrix shotshells, bismuth costs a bit more compared with steel; however, as those who have had the opportunity to work with bismuth in the field will attest, the results are more than worth the small additional cost.

Of special note here is the fact that the Bismuth Cartridge Company is the only company to offer nontoxics in all five bores, 28-gauge and .410 caliber included. Unique rounds, such as a 2½-inch 12-gauge shotshell and a 2⅞-inch 10-gauge round, are also available.

Environ-Metal's Hevi-Shot: In terms of a nontoxic alternative to lead, it's hard to do better than Environ-

Metal's revolutionary and popular blend of tungsten, iron, and nickel known as Hevi-Shot. Twenty times harder than its toxic counterpart and 10 percent more dense, Hevi-Shot hits with authority and patterns like nobody's business. For the 12-bore shooter, 2¾-inch shotshells are available; those who enjoy a light 20-gauge will find 3-inch rounds in shot sizes No. 4 through No. 7.5. All make exceptional pheasant loads. And when that big drake mallard jumps from the willow-draped inside bend of Big Walnut Creek during a mid-November bird hunt . . . let's just say it's "lights out, Mister Greenhead." But Hevi-Shot comes at a price . . . literally. At from $1.75 to $2 per round— that's *per shell!*—it's not the type of thing you want to haul out onto the trap range. Still, if it improves your bottom line, which is birds in the bag, then perhaps it's worth it, eh?

High velocity: High-velocity shotshells—say, anything over 1,300 feet per second in a field load—are quite trendy, but are they necessary? If you're shooting lead, probably not. That said, though, a little extra *z-i-n-g* on those BBs certainly isn't going to hurt.

Speed kills, regardless of whether the target's a November rooster or a December greenhead.

These quick-stepping lead pellets pack a little more punch, and they're going to get to that bird a little more quickly. Increased speed, then, provides a little cushion for those who are a bit slower on the draw. Not much, but some. High-velocity shotshells, too, are thought to help shooters hit birds up front, where all the important things—heart, lungs, and brain—are located. So in these regards, speed's a good thing.

Now, when you're talking lightweight steel pellets and roosters, high-velocity ammunition is practically a given. Sure, you're not going to need it on every flush, but then again, there are going to be those days when the birds could be brought to bag with lead No. 6s, steel No. 6s, or a broom handle . . . take your pick. My point is this: Steel, though ten times as hard as lead, is only 70 percent as dense. Therefore, those additional 150 to 200 feet per second packed into each high-velocity steel shotshell are really going to help compensate for the lower density.

GUN AND AMMO ESSENTIALS

There you have it, folks. That's a lot of words (more than 5,000, but who's counting) to say essentially these few things:

- Find a gun you're comfortable with—one that exudes confidence, one that you can become, well, *one* with.
- Get the best and the best-performing shotshells that you can get your hands on, and then familiarize yourself with them. It makes no sense to wait all year for opening day, or to drive 630 miles for that once-in-a-lifetime wild pheasant hunt in South Dakota, and fill your pet over/under or autoloader with the least expensive ammunition you could find simply because it was cheap.
- Practice. Practice some more. Then go shoot trap or skeet or sporting clays or pigeons. You owe it to yourself, and you owe that much and more to the ring-necked pheasant.

Safety in the uplands

Maybe gun safety in the pheasant fields should go without saying; however, I'm going to say it—*gun* and *safety*. In fact, let's take the subject of gun safety a step further and review the commandments of gun handling safety as they apply to pheasant hunting.

Thou shalt treat every shotgun as if loaded: If you don't know, don't guess; open the damn thing up and see for yourself if there are live rounds in it. Never assume that the gun you're being handed is empty.

Thou shalt unload before crossing: This isn't stressed enough. I don't care if it's a road ditch, creek bank, barbed-wire fence, whatever. It only takes a minute to take the shells out, cross, and load up again. You climb a fence with a loaded gun, and you're just asking to be the recipient of a traumatic experience.

Thou shalt wear blaze orange: A blaze orange hat is best. I don't know how many times a rooster has flushed, and as I'm raising the gun, I catch a glimpse of orange out of the corner of my eye . . . and the gun goes down. Orange saves lives—wear it.

Thou shalt know where thine partners are: Stay in line, stay in line, stay in line. Insist that your colleagues wear blaze orange caps and periodically look around you. Know where those other folks are.

Thou shalt use BUT not unquestionably trust your shotgun's safety: What do the guy who told me, "I don't use my safety; it takes too long to get it off," and the fellow who said, "I always hunt with the safety off; my finger acts as a safety," have in common? I only hunted with them *once*. Use your safety, but realize that it is a mechanical device that can and sometimes does fail.

Thou shalt not mix ammunition: If you, like I do, shoot a 12- 16-, and 20-gauge interchangeably throughout the season, be certain to empty your vest of the smaller shotshells—ALL of them—before filling the vest with the larger.

Thou shalt possess AND use common sense: Some of the most intelligent folks I know lack common sense; chances are you know people like this. These people shouldn't have guns, or at least not guns and ammunition. Use common sense.

Forget everything else, if you must, but never forget that gun safety, both in and out of the field, is paramount.

CHAPTER 4

The Well-Dressed Pheasant Hunter

THOSE OF YOU WHO HAVE SPENT TIME WITH me in the uplands know that my pheasant breeches are a bit, well, tattered around the edges. And though I have half a dozen perfectly good, new-in-the-box hunting boots sitting on the shelf downstairs, the ones I'll inevitably be wearing look as though they went one-on-one with a Milwaukee Sawzall . . . and lost. As for my hats and coats, let's just say that the hats are favorites, which means that they are often just a little ragged, and the coats—most long-lived Carhartts—have seen more than their fair share of field time.

And that's one of the things that I absolutely love about pheasant hunting. You can pull an outfit off the rack at your nearest Salvation Army Thrift Store and hit the field. Or you can quick-draw your credit card while thumbing through the latest issue of *Gray's Sporting Journal* and clothe yourself in some of the finest oilcloth, leather, and canvas that money—often quite a bit of money—can buy. But that's just my point. It really doesn't matter, and it matters a whole hell of a lot less to that cackling rooster whether you're wearing $300 chaps or a moth-mutilated Mickey Mouse sweatshirt. It just doesn't matter.

That said, however, and while I probably fall somewhere in between the Salvation Army and *Gray's* apparel, there are some fashion matters that

Just enough, but not too much—you want to be comfortable. That's the key to dressing for success afield.

you pheasant hunters might want to bless with some thought. Things that can not only make your outing more comfortable and thus more enjoyable, but also actually contribute to your success and effectiveness as a hunter-gatherer. Of roosters, that is.

BREECHES

Though I'm not going to be so bold as to say I've worn it all, I have, over the years, worn what I'll risk calling a wide variety of breeches while in the pursuit of ringnecks. These have ranged from blue jeans to fancy oilcloth pants that function well and look good but also have their downsides.

Is there a bottom line when it comes to deciding on pheasant-hunting breeches? If there were, it would be—*cliché warning*—you get exactly what you pay for. If you're only willing to spend $8 on a pair of second-hand cotton jeans, my guess is that eventually you're going to be cold, wet, and briar-torn well in advance of the season's end. On the other hand, simply because a pair of pants set you back $150 doesn't mean that you're getting the *perfect* upland pants. Do the *perfect* upland pants exist? Maybe and maybe not. Some are going to be better than others, and though price can and often does make a difference, it's not the only variable. Read on. . . .

Just what is available to the pheasant hunter looking to open his or her wallet on new upland pants? First, let's define just what constitutes upland pants— that is, something suitable for the pheasant hunter that might serve double duty should that person also pursue rabbits, quail, grouse, woodcock, or the like. Traditionally, good upland pants should have the following characteristics:

- *Ruggedness and durability:* Dress slacks aren't going to cut it here. Often pheasant hunters find themselves in some of the most inhospitable country known to man. Multiflora roses and blackberry bushes are anything but forgiving. Upland pants are typically subjected to all sorts of environmental abuse, and with that in mind, you're going to want to consider as rugged a material and as durable a manufacturing style as you can afford. Translation: You want something tough, such as canvas, oilcloth, or Cordura nylon. At the very least, the front panels of the pants should be covered or reinforced, as

should the back panels from the calf down to the hem, minimum. I've had both, full canvas or what-have-you and half-canvas. I find that full canvas, oilcloth, or Cordura, once broken in slightly, perform quite well *and* are as comfortable as my well-worn blue jeans. As for manufacturing style, are they double-stitched where they need to be double-stitched? Are there rivets for strength where there need to be rivets? Are the pockets well sewn *and*

Upland breeches come in a wide variety of styles, materials, and price ranges. Remember, though, you get what you pay for.

deep enough to keep your Swiss Army knife and your change from falling into the grass? Take your time, look them over, and be prepared to spend roughly $35 to $100 for a pair that's going to last you more than one season. And note that, please—*more than one season.*

• *Comfort:* There's nothing that says your brush pants can't be comfortable. To that end, make sure you try

them on—even if you're absolutely sure you have a 36-inch waist and a 34-inch inseam. Do they fit well, and not only that, are they comfortable? And while you're at it, take another look at how they're made. Are the hems stitched well and look as though they'll hold up to the constant abuse you're going to give them? The hems, by the way, are going to be one of the first places to wear, so take a second look at those. Chances are you're not going to be wearing these breeches out on the town (well, maybe you are), but there is no reason for them to be uncomfortable. With luck, you'll be wearing them quite a bit. Know what I mean?

- *Suspender buttons:* Okay, so you haven't worn suspenders since a friend got you a pair of those rainbow-colored ones back in the mid-1970s. That notwithstanding, I'd strongly suggest getting upland pants that come complete with suspender buttons. Granted, you might not wear them, but it's one of those things where it's better to have them and not need them than to need them and not have them. Suspenders are a good thing . . . even the rainbow-colored ones.

- *Lined or unlined:* This is a judgment call on your part based, understandably, on where you're going to be doing the better part of your pheasant hunting. I've never owned lined or insulated upland breeches for a couple reasons. First, unlined pants

are going to be less expensive than lined ones, and I can always, and often do, wear thermal, polypropylene, or synthetic pants underneath. And second, unless you're doing the majority of your pheasant hunting under brutally cold conditions, lined pants are invariably going to prove rather warm, especially once you start doing any amount of walking.

As for what's available in terms of the actual material from which the breeches are fashioned:

- *Denim (blue jeans):* Good if they're absolutely all you have; however, cotton jeans don't provide much in the way of protection from briars and other stickers. They aren't waterproof and are downright cold, especially if they're wet. I'd try something else.
- *Canvas:* Probably the most traditional material from which upland pants are made, canvas isn't tremendous in terms of warmth, but it's great when it comes to saving your hide from rosebushes, barbed-wire fences, and other nasties. Today canvas upland pants are available in both waxed and unwaxed versions. Waxing simply makes the pants waterproof; however, waxed canvas pants require maintenance and upkeep, otherwise known as rewaxing. I've worn both and prefer the unwaxed pants.
- *Cordura nylon:* A relatively new material, Cordura is the same stuff that your new knife sheath is made of or your new boots are covered in. Typically, upland pants that use Cordura as a covering will be what I call half pants; that is, the front from the hips down and the back from the calf down will be protected with nylon, while the rest of the pants will be made of traditional cotton jean or canvas material. On the ruggedness scale, it's tough to beat Cordura. The same can't be said about the material's waterproof characteristics, though it certainly does help slow what's known as the Getting Soaked process.
- *Oilcloth:* One of the country's best-known makers of oilcloth upland pants and other gear is the Seattle-based C. C. Filson Company. I took to wearing their oilcloth upland pants a couple years back and

One pair of canvas pants (left), and one pair of oilcloth. As long as your breeches are rugged, durable, and comfortable, the material really doesn't matter.

have been very pleased with their performance in the field. True, the waxy coating from which the pants derive their name needs periodic upkeep. And also true, when worn under warm conditions *and* with no barrier between yourself and the pants, these oilcloth breeches seem almost to melt slightly on your skin. These things being said, however, oilcloth is a very rugged and protective material that seems, at least by my testing, to stand up well to hard use. It's a bit more expensive than the other materials, but remember what I said about getting what you pay for?

Given the wide variety of upland pants available today, how do you decide what you're going to need? This one's actually quite easy, once you consider several questions. How often are you going to hunt? Under what conditions, both cover and weather, will you most often be out? Will it be cold? Warm? Warm and cold, off and on? Will canvas work based on the fact that there aren't many briars, or would oilcloth or Cordura serve you better? Once you start looking closely at both where and how you hunt, the answers to your questions regarding brush pants—aka upland breeches—are going to practically fall into your lap . . . no pun intended.

CHAPS

Chaps are closely related to breeches and serve the same purpose whether worn by a Harley rider, a cowboy, or a pheasant hunter—to protect the wearer's legs. Some chaps are made of leather, but today's upland chaps are typically made of canvas, Cordura, or oilcloth. Several nice things about chaps, aside from the fact that they protect your person from ankle to hip, are that they're comparatively cool, even under the most extreme hunting conditions; easy to put on and take off; comfortable and very rugged; and usually $10 to $20 less expensive than traditional full upland pants.

SHIRTS AND SWEATERS

Depending on the day, the weather, and my mood, I can be found each fall gunning roosters in everything from a favorite U.S. Marine Corps T-shirt to a fancy, orange-elbowed Columbia Sharptail shooting shirt . . . and everything in between. The fact is that it really doesn't matter what the shirt, or even the lack thereof—only

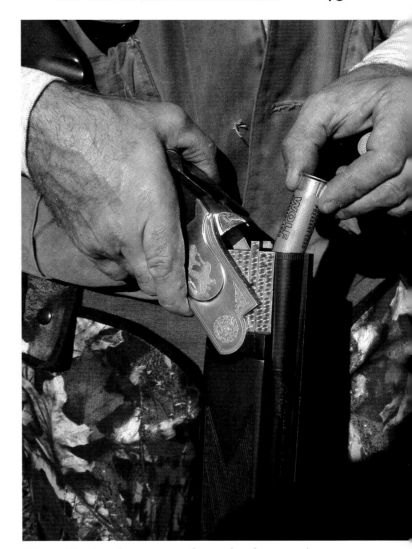

Chaps, like those here, are another option for protecting your legs in the field.

that you're comfortable, protected from the elements or environments, and look as good as you think you need to look.

That said, what do I wear into the field when the topic is roosters? During the early season and even into the middle parts, I can typically be seen wearing a Columbia Sharptail-esque type of shooting shirt. The long sleeves, complete with their reinforced forearms and shooting shoulders, protect my arms from scratches and scrapes and help keep me warm during that chilly first hour or so in the morning. Plus, they do all that without binding me up or being uncomfortable to the point that it affects my shooting. Such shirts, too, being made from a cotton canvas material, are cool in the heat and yet can be combined with an appropriate

Above: A fashion plate? No, but on this mild eastern Iowa morning, a short-sleeved sweatshirt and vest were more than enough.
Right: Fancy or simple, a hunting coat's primary function is just that—functionality. Find one that fits and works for your purposes.

undershirt—a synthetic or thermal, perhaps—should the weather turn a bit cold. The longer tails of such upland shirts stay tucked in, and overall they look good, especially for photographs. Lined and unlined versions are both available, and prices range from $25 to $50, depending on the make, model, and manufacturer.

So what if it's a little cooler—say, November in Iowa or South Dakota? What should you consider in terms of upper body coverage? In years past, I'd go to a warm hunting coat; however, I've all but forsaken the traditional hunting or upland coat, opting instead for one or several layers consisting of thermals, polypropylene, or other synthetics. On most cold-weather hunts, I'll start with a polypropylene short-sleeved undershirt. This helps retain heat while allowing moisture in the form of perspiration to escape away from my skin. The polypro shirt is followed by either one or two long-sleeved Carhartt thermal tops, depending on the

conditions. Next, I add a black U.S. military wool sweater—tight but not uncomfortable or binding. And finally, I top the layers off with a wonderfully warm C. C. Filson wool shooting sweater in olive drab. Trust me, both the military and the Filson sweaters are a pain to wash and dry without their coming out sized only for Barbie's friend, Ken. But this is the best combination of cold-weather clothing I've hit upon—bar none—in terms of warmth, comfort, protection, and ease of movement.

COATS

When I was growing up, pheasant hunting meant a canvas coat that had seen more than its fair share of field time. After years of being dragged through the briars, goldenrod, and countless other brushy things, the bottom hem of the coat and the cuffs were hopelessly frayed. The coat itself was soiled—not filthy,

One of the nicest gentlemen we've had the pleasure of spending time with afield, Bill Costner opts for a basic blaze orange hooded sweatshirt and vest instead of coat.

I like my Winchester coat. It's big enough so I can swing a gun comfortably, but doesn't fall around me like a heavy blanket.

but traditionally unclean. The pockets were filled with weed seeds and MoonPie wrappers, and the slightly bloodstained game bag showed a ragged hole in one corner. V-shaped tears, trademark barbed-wire rips, graced one elbow and the exact center of the back. Hanging there the night before opening day, the coat truly was a thing of beauty.

The dress back then consisted of brush pants, shell vest with a double row of loops, and the requisite unlined heavy canvas coat. Ah, the day my Aunt Jean gave me the Carhartt coat that belonged to my late Uncle Tom, a longtime telephone lineman. With that gift, my upland wardrobe was complete . . . or as complete as it gets for a fourteen-year-old.

Today I don't see a lot of hunting coats in the field. Whereas back in the day everyone wore them, now I'd feel pretty safe in saying that perhaps half, if that, of the folks afield chasing pheasants don the old canvas coats. In milder weather, they wear shooting shirts and vests that double as shell carrier and game bag. Cooler

temperatures will see more layers—sweaters are common—but only under extreme conditions will today's pheasant hunter resort to wrapping himself in a full-length canvas coat. It's too bad, really, for the coats, I always thought, were part of the mystique.

Nostalgia behind us, there are plenty of fine hunting coats available today for those who might want them. The big mail-order houses—Bass Pro Shops and Cabela's—both have their own lines of upland gear, coats included. The Seattle-based C. C. Filson Company makes a tremendous oilcloth coat that's built to last *and* withstand the 1,001 types of abuse we pheasant hunters throw at our clothing. Winchester, Columbia, and Browning, all recognized companies, offer traditional upland hunting coats with as many bells and whistles—zip-off sleeves, speed-loading shell loops, hydration systems, removable game bags, and so on—as you might want or hope to have.

I have two rules of thumb when shopping for an upland coat. First, find one that fits comfortably, allowing freedom of movement and ease of swing. Lord knows you don't need any more excuses for missing your fourth rooster of the morning. While you're trying coats on, make sure it's going to fit over a light shirt *and* a heavier sweater. This leads us to the second consideration: Find a coat that fits the weather conditions in which you're most likely to be hunting. Do you need a lined coat, or will an unlined model work just fine? Maybe you want to consider something like Columbia's Ptarmigan X Upland Parka, which features a zip-out fleece liner. At $150, the Ptarmigan isn't inexpensive, but it's a tough garment that is designed to last and can serve you throughout the whole season, warm and cold.

UPLAND VESTS

Despite what I just said in the paragraphs above—and the fact that it is a blow to tradition—I seldom wear a hunting coat anymore when I'm chasing ringnecks. Maybe it's psychological, but I feel less confined (wow . . . talk about seeing your shrink here, eh?) when I'm wearing just a shirt or sweater with a shooting vest over top.

Hunting vests serve three primary purposes. First, they protect you somewhat from the elements and the nasty things, such as wild rosebushes, that you spend the better part of pheasant season walking through. Second, there's the safety factor, as most vests are at least in part blaze orange, required by law for upland game hunters in most states. And third, they're the canvas equivalent of a support vehicle—a combination shell holder, game carrier, and transporter of water bottles, cell phones, leashes, dog treats, candy bars, oatmeal cakes, and any of a hundred other things we find fit to burden ourselves with.

Two basic types of hunting vests exist: the traditional model, with what I'll call full shoulders, and the strap vest version. I wear a full-shouldered Filson oilcloth model all season long, regardless of the weather. In October and early November, it tops a light, long-sleeved hunting shirt; come December, a wool Filson vest over a couple layers of thermal or polypropylene serves as a foundation. My wife, on the other hand, prefers an oilcloth strap-style vest. This, she says, can more easily be worn over a heavier coat and offers the same conveniences as my full vest. I've worn both styles, and though I can't say anything negative about the strap vest, I just prefer the full-shouldered model.

You may have noticed a common denominator in much of the upland clothing: oilcloth. To be more correct, the cotton fabric, at least in the case of the Filson items I wear, is known as Tin Cloth. The material has been coated with a special oil-finish wax, thus making it extremely water repellent and wind resistant. Don't get me wrong; traditional heavy canvas as found in any of the popular Carhartt garments works just fine afield. This waxed cotton fabric, though, is very low maintenance, incredibly rugged, and offers great protection from briars. And, fashion plate that I am, I like the fact that it looks really, really good in front of the camera. Yes, such vests and coats come at a price, but quality usually does.

Vests should be comfortable but provide enough pocket space for the long list of things pheasant hunters carry into—and hopefully out of—the field.

Inside the upland vest

Some folks wear upland vests, some don't. I wouldn't be without mine, and I'll tell you exactly why: I carry a lot of stuff. Doesn't matter if I'm pheasant hunting, turkey hunting, wet-wading a creek for smallmouth, or walking to the neighborhood store, it seems I'm always carrying something. And if I didn't carry it into the field, I'm hoping that by the end of the day, I'm carrying something—anything—out of the field.

Let me give you a glimpse, albeit brief, at the contents of my upland vest. Before I do, however, let me

just say that everything here is indeed absolutely necessary. It really is . . .

Shotshells: A given. A pheasant hunt without shotshells is just another walk in the weeds.

Leash: I prefer a tight link metal model with a sturdy handle for the Labs. Sometimes I clip it around my waist so it's handy rather than put it in a vest pocket, but I've been told I look reminiscent of the Village People. Do we want to go there?

Water: Hot or cold weather, I always carry water. Usually a couple 16-ounce plastic bottles is enough for me and the dogs.

Granola bars: Fudge-coated chewy chocolate chip. They're quick-energy food.

Dog treats: Two or three Purina ProPlan brand performance bars, a nutritional supplement that keeps the dogs happy, healthy, and running well.

First-aid kit: In a small, hard case, one of those travel bar soap containers that cost $1, I carry Visine, aspirin or ibuprofen, tweezers, MedGel, Bactine, six to eight bandages, a small mirror, Chapstick, dental floss, and about three feet of strong nylon decoy cord. You'd be amazed at how often this stuff comes in handy, and it's all lightweight and hardly noticeable . . . unless you need it and don't have it.

Shooting glasses: Never used to carry them, but I do now. And I even use them.

Permission slips and business cards: Some states, Ohio for instance, require hunters on private ground to have in possession signed permission slips from the landowners. If that's the case, they're in a Ziploc bag in my chest vest pocket. As for business cards—well, you might not have them; however, they're not a bad idea and are great for leaving with landowners on whose land you'd like to hunt. Keep them simple: name, address, phone, e-mail, vehicle description, and plate number perhaps.

Jet gets a well-deserved break and half a Purina Performance Bar during an October hunt in South Dakota.

Upland vests are a carry-all, quite similar to the spring turkey hunter's vest.

A beautiful picture—oh, and the vest. Get yourself a good quality vest.

You're putting a lot of stock in what you put on your feet. Get the best boots
you can afford and try them on before you buy.

FOOTWEAR

The infantryman lives and dies by his feet. Hobble the feet, and you've hobbled the man. Such also could be said for the pheasant hunter.

I could (trust me!) talk for hours on this boot and that boot, discussing all of the positives and negatives connected with a certain tread design or material or boot height or this or that . . . but I won't. Why the brevity? The fact is, choosing pheasant footwear is all about fit and comfort. Anything beyond that is, as the man who tried to sell us $23,000 worth of siding called it, gingerbread. Accessories, that's what I'm saying.

Find a boot that fits. Find a boot that's comfortable. Chances are you're going to pay $100, give or take, for these boots, but that's okay. Would you rather drop a C-note on quality boots that you can

wear for five to ten years, depending on how often you hunt, or a $20 bill on a cheap pair of blister factories? It's just that simple. Take care of your new boots according to the manufacturer's recommendations. And by all means, get good socks. A good boot with worthless socks means you might as well be walking the fields barefoot. Bottom line? Try them out in the store, ask questions of the clerk, and break them in prior to opening day. Wait until day one to wear your new clogs, and you deserve sore feet.

A couple things before we leave the subject of footwear. The first is the question of deciding between leather and one of the new synthetic materials such as Cordura or Gore-Tex. Leather, let me say, is fantastic. It looks good, it wears well, and there are few things

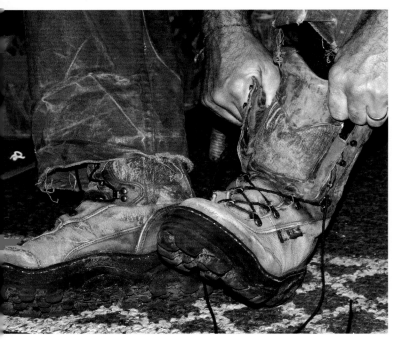

These Rocky boots have seen a thousand miles and are just now getting broken in. Quality and comfort come at a price, but it's a price you should be willing to pay.

What you put on your head is your choice. Note the shooting (safety) glasses, an excellent idea whenever working with firearms.

as comfortable as a broken-in leather boot; however, leather does require care and upkeep, both to keep it clean and to ensure that it stays water resistant. The synthetics, on the other hand, call for little maintenance, are generally waterproof, and, should you care, come in any number of camouflage patterns. The synthetics, particularly those that incorporate materials such as Gore-Tex or Thinsulate, can also be warmer than a leather boot—a plus for the cold-weather uplander—but are cold feet really a concern for the hunter in constant motion? Leather, synthetic, warmth, it's your call.

Finally, there's boot height and tread design. Currently, I switch back and forth between boots from Rocky and Danner, both of which fall into the eight-to nine-inch-tall category. I like higher boots for both the ankle support and the added protection or padding they offer. Other folks prefer ankle-high boots, saying they're more comfortable and cool. The key word here is *comfort*. Height is a personal matter; comfort applies to all boots. Tread design is another personal choice. Chances are the area or areas you frequently hunt will determine the type of tread design you both want and need. I don't like an aggressive tread on my pheasant

boots. A wedge or similarly mild tread provides ample traction but avoids picking up mud and tracking it into the house.

HEADGEAR AND GLOVES

Two final clothing-related items and we'll call the chapter a wrap. On the subject of hats or headgear, that's easy: Wear what's comfortable and what the weather dictates. For all but the most extreme conditions, I'll wear a simple blaze orange ball cap. If the temperature is above, say, 50 degrees F, a lightweight synthetic-cotton blend cap does fine; below 50 and I'm starting to consider a similarly light cover lined with Thinsulate or Gore-Tex for additional warmth and wind-blocking capabilities. Saddle cloth and a material called Ten Mile Cloth are both lightweight, come lined or unlined, and are softer, more comfortable alternatives to the traditional poly-synthetic caps.

Now if it's downright cold, I'll trade the ball cap for a wool or wool-blend watch cap—or as the Canadians say, a toque. Even though pheasant hunting involves a goodly amount of walking, there's still plenty of opportunity to lose precious body heat via the top of your head. Enter a heat-loss preventative watch cap. My personal favorite is a wool cap. Color: blaze orange. A bit on the small side, the toque can be worn more like a skullcap, my thinking here being that I don't want material over top my ears that might interfere in any way with my hearing. Maybe it's an insignificant detail, purely psychological or flat-out anal retentive, this hat-over-the-ears thing, but I know each fall I hear enough flushes before I actually see the rooster to make this a factor to be considered.

Then there are the gloves. I seldom wear gloves while wing shooting. I don't care how thin they are or how little loss of manual dexterity the advertisements claim, I just don't feel comfortable wearing gloves. My personal exception to this rule comes, not surprisingly, when the Iowa winter turns downright nasty and the mercury plummets into Mother Nature's basement. Under these conditions, I'll don a pair of fingerless rag-wool gloves—fingerless so as not to deviate from my "feel the trigger and the safety" philosophy, and rag wool for its warmth, even when damp with frost or snow or whatever.

But that's just me. There are a lot of uplanders who wouldn't think about heading afield during early fall or winter without some type of gloves in their side pocket, and fortunately for them, there are plenty of hand coverings to choose from. A quick look in the Cabela's catalog or a run through "shooting gloves" using your favorite Internet search engine will reveal mitts ranging from kangaroo hide—Thinsulate-lined, nonetheless—shooting gloves to those made of neoprene, cowhide, and a host of other materials. Traditional brown jersey gloves? Chances are you can find them at your local convenience store and they'll set you back only $1.09 or so, meaning you're not going to be disappointed when you lose them, the Lab eats them, or both.

What type or style of glove to wear while gunning roosters is a personal decision. One factor that applies, however, whether your hand covers are fashioned from cotton or kangaroo: practice. My advice is to find a pair of gloves sometime during the warmer months, and then shoot a round of trap, skeet, or sporting clays with gloves on. Is it strange to shoot with mitts on in the middle of August? Who cares. 'Tis better to find out in advance of the season that the gloves you selected don't perform as expected—too tight, too loose, can't feel the trigger, slippery, or any of a dozen

I prefer fingerless rag-wool gloves that keep my hands warm. Tip: Try the gloves on the shooting range during the off-season.

other variables—than to suffer cold, naked, or possibly even unsafe paws on a mid-November hunt.

Two final words for those who find themselves afield during the latter part of the season with nothing but blocks of numb below the wrists: chemical handwarmers. They're cheap, they're lightweight, and they work wonders—an amazing tool that costs only 99 cents.

CHAPTER 5

The Pheasant Hunter's Best Friend

A GOOD FRIEND CALLED YESTERDAY—AN English setter-owning friend, by the way— to tell me the news. "It looks," he said, the excitement obvious in his voice, "like I'm going to get a six-month-old German wirehair pup. This friend of ours, she . . . " and he rambled on and on and on. Dogs, even the prospects of one, will do that to a man.

Let me first say that I wasn't raised by a bird dog-owning man. No, my family raised and owned beagles, some of which would, on those few and far between days when we would actually encounter a pheasant in northeast Ohio, chase it—sometimes even into the air. Should the bird be a rooster and the shot true, the dog—Nellie, Spike, Jeb, Missy, Mitzy, or any of the other tricolored hounds—would give the bundle of feathers a nuzzle, perhaps even a shake or two, and then go back about the business for which they had been bred, namely, chasing rabbits. No, back then, bird dogs were something that the Other Guy had.

Today, some thirty years and many a beagle dog later, things around the Johnson household are a little different. My wife and I currently have not one or two black dogs—Labs, that is—but three. Mama, Jet, and son Deacon are papered clear back roughly to the creation of the universe. It's a good thing, the paperwork, I guess, but so far in our limited experience, it hasn't proved absolutely necessary in terms

Richard Kieffer of Kieffer's Pheasant Hunting in White Lake, South Dakota, and Ebony.
Nah, he doesn't like that dog much, now does he?

of their performance in the field or the joy we get from simply having the black dogs—the Dogs of Terror, as a pheasant hunting friend once called them—around. And Maggie? Twelve-year-old Maggie is just Maggie—part pit bull, part Chow, and part papered Labrador retriever, or at least that's what the lady claimed. I hadn't wanted a dog that day in Washington, or any day for that matter, but Julie had the Heinz 57 pup wrapped up in her arms, and I feared, as many a man has, that I was too late to circumvent the inevitable. "How much, ma'am?" I asked, hoping that the price would squelch the deal. "Oh, no, honey," she said. "You folks go on and take that pup. Won't cost you a thing."

Well, let me tell you something, though I'm sure some of you already know this: There's no such thing as a free dog. But there she was, a little black shaking ball of fur with a speckled tongue and awfully big feet. A dozen years later, Maggie has flushed and retrieved everything from roosters to rails to prairie chickens, and I wouldn't take a million dollars cash money for her gray face and round ol' belly. No, sir. I'd give you a body part before I'd give you Miss Maggie.

Dogs, it seems, will do that to a man.

WHY A PHEASANT DOG?
The first thing that comes to my mind is *Why not a pheasant dog?,* but it's a terrible thing to answer a question with a question. That said, let's take a look at what a canine assistant can bring to the pheasant hunter's table.

Find 'em and Flush 'em
This probably can go without saying, but I'll say it anyway: To shoot roosters, you must first find roosters. And once you've found them, and unless you're going to sluice them running down the cornrows like a cottontail rabbit, you have to convince them of the necessity of flight.

Enter a dog. Let's face it—you're but one person, and if you're a single male person, you've likely experienced the challenge that is finding, well, anything. Your wallet or keys come immediately to mind. Now take your single humanness and put it in a one hundred-acre field of waist-high set-aside. Add a couple dozen birds whose sole task that day is to elude you, and you start to see just how different *finding* can be

from simply *wandering around aimlessly.* Trust me, I've wandered around aimlessly more than enough to know exactly what it looks and feels like.

With a dog's eyes, ears, and phenomenal sense of smell at your side, comforting, like a furry six-shooter—well, now you're not just one guy. Before, you were a carpenter with an empty nail apron. Now you're Bob Vila with a Snap-On chest filled to overflowing with every hand tool known to man. But enough with the analogies, for here's the bottom line: A well-behaved dog with a little experience, a decent nose, and the desire to please can help you find roost-

There's really no reason to ask a pheasant hunter, "Why a dog?" It's like asking Kris Kringle why the red jumpsuit.

ers that otherwise would have gone undiscovered. It's just as simple as that.

And once that dog's found those birds that would have escaped you, its job is then to hogtie that rooster until such a time as you wander over or, as in the case of our trio of black dogs, force that otherwise ground-hugging cockbird into the air where the situation then becomes—literally—hit or miss. Find 'em and flush 'em are parts one and two of the equation.

Part three comes immediately after the shot, assuming your aim was indeed true. If your aim,

in fact, was not true, a good dog will afford you two, maybe three, bouts of forgiveness; after that, you're on your own. Don't think a pointer can give you a "just what the hell is wrong with you" look? Just miss in its presence half a dozen times; you'll be walking back to the rig alone.

Retrieving downed birds is another canine duty. Or if not retrieving, at least revealing the whereabouts of the fallen rooster in some manner. A good friend's setter will only occasionally retrieve a bird; however, Ike will find and drool on each and every bird you

Poetry in motion and when motionless. To dog men, it's all about watching 'em work.

knock down. Sure, it'll be soggy, but you'll have your rooster—and that, folks, is the desired result there.

But retrieving a dead rooster is one thing; rooting out, chasing down, and bringing back a crippled bird is a whole nother chapter. Ask one hundred avid uplanders taken to hunting with dogs, and almost to the man, if not to the man, they'll say that reducing the number of wounded and perhaps unrecoverable birds is the number one argument in favor of hunting pheasants with a dog. Bar none. Period. End of story. And I agree wholeheartedly. There is truly nothing that sickens a hunter, a true sportsman, more than losing game; to know that the shot was inadequately true and that somewhere a rooster sits, with a broken wing, a busted leg, or an eyedropper full of pellets in the flank. It does no good to seek solace in the statement, "Predators have to eat, too." That, to me, is insignificant justification for an error. A trained dog, however, can lessen the frequency with which these traumatic losses occur. End them entirely? Certainly not, for our chosen sport is not without its errors. An upgrade in personal marksmanship can help. So, too, can a reevaluation in judgment; that is, the decision regarding when to shoot or not shoot. Still, when that old cockbird slants down, a wingtip canted and running gear already in motion, you'll be thanking your lucky stars that those black

dogs or white dogs or gray dogs or speckled dogs are in your corner. Really, really lucky . . .

Finally, there's the companionship. I won't dwell long here, or at best, I'll try not to linger, but I'm not sure exactly what I'd do without Maggie or Jet or Deacon. Certainly, they're useful tools in the field—technical assistants, if you will—but as anyone who's ever owned a dog-turned-partner knows, they're much more than that. They listen when I talk. They ensure that I never have to hunt alone. They're sympathetic when I miss, or they're visually encouraging—reprimanding?—when they eventually tire of my prolonged accuracy trauma. They find my roosters, and they'll find them again on those days when my shooting is less than stellar. They'll work to the point of exhaustion and then get up to do it all again despite aches and pains and barbed-wire cuts. They'll get hair on the seat and shake in the truck. All this for the price of half a MoonPie and a scratch behind the ears . . . or in Maggie's case, a quick belly rub.

Now you tell me, where else are you going to find a bargain like that?

Facing page: Like his mama, Jet, Deacon—here with me in eastern Iowa—will point and hold as long as the bird does. A pointing Lab is a fantastic combination in my book.

Warm-Weather Canine Care

Opening weekend of pheasant season 2003 in South Dakota arrived, as it often does, with simply ridiculous numbers of roosters—and a lot of folks chasing those roosters. Unfortunately, and somewhat uncharacteristically, it also came with extraordinarily high temperatures, with some places across the state seeing readings in the upper 70s to low 80s. Roosters tumbled while men sweated and cussed and dogs died.

Yes, I said *dogs died*. Lee Harstad, media relations manager for the South Dakota Department of Tourism and State Development, explained in a note to a local newspaperman that he heard reports of "40 to 75 dogs dying, and a great many others becoming ill" because of the heat. And this was just opening weekend.

Is it inexcusable for a man to allow his dog—his hunting partner—to die from heat exhaustion? I think so. Is it irresponsible? Again, I certainly think so. Is this type of death avoidable? One more time, I believe it is.

Prevention, most physicians will tell you, traditionally begins with common sense, and that's where we'll start in the case of hunting dogs and heat. First, if it's that hot, don't take the dog. I realize that you didn't train and feed your dog for nine months only to leave it in the kennel; however, just imagine yourself draped in a full-length beaver coat running around on your hands and knees in the puckerbrush . . . *and* it's 85 degrees with 90 percent humidity. Remember, dogs are much, much shorter than you, and where they're working, there's no wind to cool them off. Instead, Rover has to pant—and pant a lot—in order to keep cool, and panting leads to an incredible loss of water.

Always, always, always make sure you have plenty of water for your dog, and offer it up often. Better yet, if possible, hunt near a creek or stop by an old stock tank or farm pond, and let the dog soak and play. "If you're going to hunt your dogs in the heat," advises Kevin Michalowski, author of *15 Minutes to a Great Dog*, "run them briefly, hunt them slow, make shade available, and always be sure to keep them—and yourself—hydrated." He says that it's important for hunters to know and recognize the symptoms of heat-related problems as they pertain to their canine assistants. "Uncontrollable panting is the first sign. Then a dazed or confused look, almost as if the dog can't think. It may not want to move." If it gets to this point, you need to get to the vet—immediately! If a vet isn't available, then cool the dog down quickly; water applied to head, neck, shoulders, and belly might help. Michalowski says, "Even if you do get the dog to the vet and they start fluids, there's no guarantee that it's going to survive. If it does survive, it may have brain damage, heart damage, or something major. It's all about prevention in the first place."

Give 'em a break every now and then. Remember, they're working a hell of a lot harder than you are.

Above: Julie and I taught our dogs—Deacon here—to drink from the bottle, which makes it simple to always have a good supply of available water on hand when hunting.
Left: Even in winter, making water available to your hound in the field is crucial.

Two of Deacon's first retrieves. I couldn't have been more proud of that big pup.

Kevin Michalowski—a good friend and tremendous trainer of dogs.

PICKING A BREED

Should you steal a glance at the sidebar titled "The Canine Assistants," (page 101) you'll see that there are ten breeds of dog commonly associated with pheasants and pheasant hunting, the dogs you're most likely to encounter on any given day in any given field. That said, I've come across folks afield accompanied by dogs that you wouldn't normally think of as pheasant hounds—chows, terriers, shepherds, bassets, and Lord only knows what else. These atypical upland dogs, it was either explained or assumed, performed as their master saw fit—and if you think about it, that's really the bottom line when it comes to choosing a breed with the task of chasing roosters in mind: What do you want the dog to do?

Take us, for example. In Maggie's case, Julie—and begrudgingly, I—simply wanted a family dog to replace an older one she'd lost in an accident. The mixed-breed Maggie was to be a pet, nothing else; to my surprise, however, she soon proved herself extremely intelligent, individually loyal, and quite capable of finding and retrieving anything and everything we decided to shoot . . . except starlings, that is. Taken with the black Lab portion of Maggie's parentage, Julie returned from a solo trip to Washington state in February 1998 with a small, black bundle in tow. Of Portland, Oregon, lineage, Jet was a full-blooded and heavily papered pup. "We can use her for pheasants and ducks and geese and everything," came my wife's explanation and justification, neither of which was really necessary, as the little girl pup was pretty to the point of no return. Two litters later in 2003, we decide to keep Deacon, our first male black Lab. "We'd better get rid of him soon," I told Julie as we tailed out the process of finding the last of Jet's eight pups new homes. "I'm getting kinda used to him." Well, we're really used to him now, and him to us.

Which brings me to this point, one that I'm sure you've already noticed—we're black Lab folks. You, on the other hand, might not be. Maybe you're more a pointer person. Maybe you prefer something smaller. Or an indoor dog. Or an outdoor dog. Or a family pet *and* a hunter. Whatever the case may be, I'm sure there's a pheasant dog out there built to suit you. But which one? There are several factors that you should consider to help you decide.

Time Available

Here's one of the most important questions, if not *the* most important question, to ask yourself: How much time do I have to devote to a dog? And that's not just hunting time. In addition to field time, there's training time, time away from the dog, and what I'll call socialization time, or one-on-one bonding time. How much time you have to devote to a bird dog can certainly help determine what breed might be best, but even more, the answer can reveal whether you should even have a dog in the first place. Face it, some folks simply

shouldn't have them. Dogs, like children, are a huge responsibility; they're an investment—something in which you invest yourself in order to see a return, be that return field performance, security, friendship, loyalty, or ideally all four.

How much time hunters spend with their future pheasant dog depends entirely on what they expect that dog to become in the field. If they are happy with basic performance, then the time spent will be limited. Conversely, if they want a field-trial-caliber dog, they will have to devote more time to training.

Okay, so let's say that you have the time, and you've accepted the fact that dog ownership is a responsibility. How much does the amount of time you realistically have to give your new partner affect breed choice? For some answers I went to good friend, dog trainer, and author Kevin Michalowski. Mick trains and shows a preference for yellow Labs and does a right fine job in their education. Since 2002, the young man has authored two superb books on the subject of training pups and adult dogs, the aptly named *15 Minutes to*

A pair of up-and-comers in Plankinton, South Dakota. They'll have the program down next fall.

a Great Dog and its companion, *15 Minutes to a Great Puppy.* Kevin knows dogs, so it was with this in mind that I asked him for his recommendations.

"For the hunter with only *some* time," Kevin says, "a Labrador retriever would be a good choice. A Lab will find and retrieve a ton of pheasants with just the basic commands—come, sit, down, fetch. Of course, you can invest the time and take that Lab to the next level—steady to the flush, for instance, field trials, that sort of thing. But a well-bred Lab given the basics can do just fine.

"For the hunter with a little more time," Kevin continues, "a springer spaniel is an excellent choice. Like the Labs, they can make fine pheasant dogs given only the basics. In fact, if you teach a springer to come every time it's called, it will learn quickly to find a dead bird. The dog may not deliver the bird to hand immediately, but a springer will find it. Springers, too, have more energy than Labs. At the end of the day, when the Lab's walking and has had enough, a springer's still bouncing around and ready to go. They're more active than labs, but not as enthusiastic or exuberant as, say, one of the pointers. You can spend a little more time with a spaniel. Teach it to be steady at the flush—that is, to sit prior to the shot, and this takes some time to teach—and you'll have a great pheasant dog.

"Any of the pointing breeds take more time," Kevin says. "They're active dogs, big movers. They cover lots of ground, which can be a good thing in places like South Dakota or Kansas or Nebraska. But that also means they're going to need more time, dedication, and determination on your part. The pointers, like the others, need the basics, but they need training above and beyond that—whoa, steady at the flush, steady with groups of birds. Too, they can have attitudes around other dogs, and you need to set time aside to deal with that potentiality. Pointers are the athletes of the dog world, and as such, they can require a great deal of time."

Dog Size and Where You Live

The size of a breed at adulthood and your living quarters also play into the equation. Granted, there can and often do exist large, medium, and smaller varieties of the same breed, and you might want to consider this as you're making your decision. Across the board, how-

He really doesn't look like he's enjoying what I'm handing out, does he?

ever, there are big dogs and smaller dogs. Deacon, our two-year-old male black Lab, weighs in at right around one hundred pounds. Labs need to run in order to be happy. They need to dig and roll and chase critters; essentially, they need room to play. Thus a Lab probably wouldn't be a good choice should you live in a small studio apartment in the middle of the city. Likewise, Julie's Deacon wouldn't get the nod if you're looking for something a little smaller. Or that isn't capable of eating two goats and a chicken each morning. Or a hound whose "eliminations" don't rival a 1969 Volkswagen Beetle in size.

All hunting dogs—hell, all dogs for that matter—need room to run. Your ground, rented ground, state ground, city ground . . . it doesn't matter. Take a look around. How much room do you have to offer a dog? This look around can help you decide not only what type of pheasant dog is best for you, but also whether a dog is a good idea in the first place.

I was going to wait to address this, but I'll go ahead and tend to it right now rather briefly. I'll call it the "indoor dog/outdoor dog controversy." There are folks who claim that a hunting dog can't be an indoor dog and an indoor dog can't be a hunting dog. Rather, an indoor dog is a pet, whereas an outside dog can be, though isn't necessarily, a hunting dog. Now bear with me as I try to find the right words here . . . That's bullshit. I have, as you may have too, seen indoor dogs—Phil Bourjaily's setter Ike is a fine example—that have been tremendous pheasant dogs. Maggie, Jet, and Deacon spend at least half their time indoors, and they're excellent pheasant finders. True, I'm biased, but they're still very good. Steve Hickoff's setters, Radar, Midge, and Jenny? Inside dogs all, and they're wonderful field performers. Now conversely, you can have an outside dog—with the kennel and the bark and the whole nine yards—that isn't worth a damn in the field.

I don't think indoors versus outdoors has anything to do with how a dog performs in the field. I think it has to do with breeding, first, and the owner, second. Or rather, the owner's willingness—key word: willingness—and ability to teach that dog to do what he wants that dog to do. I will say this, though: The fact that our Labs are indoor people dogs for much of the year, that they ride with us on the front seat of the truck, go with us when we go fishing, go on vacation with us, and spend 365 days a year with us, has allowed us to bond deeply with them, and them with us. They know when they've done something wrong, and they know when they've done something right. And I don't believe I'm wrong here when I say that all three of them have a strong desire to please Julie and me. They *want* to do well in the field, and I think that desire has much of its foundations in the fact that we spend so much time together.

Need more convincing on the subject of an indoor hunting dog? You ask the neighborhood kids why, during the winter, Jet sleeps on a blanket upstairs to the west side of my bed. "To keep the ghosts away," they'll tell you, referring to the spirits that inhabit our 1897-model two-story rural schoolhouse. And who am I to disagree, eh?

Utility or Versatility

Essentially, what do you want to do with the dog? Rather, what do you want to hunt? If it's strictly pheasants you're after, then maybe a pointer would be best. Roosters, doves, and other assorted upland birds?

The Other Hunter's Dog

Sooner or later, if you haven't already, you'll have the opportunity to gun over another man's dog. Over the years, I've had the great fortune of hunting with a number of ladies and gentlemen who possessed extraordinary canine assistants—and the great misfortune of spending time afield with dogs better suited to life on a couch, far away from anything even remotely resembling a pheasant and a shotgun.

Shooting over another man's dog can prove a most memorable experience; however, there are some things you should know and remember should the opportunity to do so present itself. And this reminder, surprisingly enough, applies even to those of you who own sporting dogs, for I've seen some of the worst behavior regarding another hunter's hound coming from dog people themselves. No one, it would seem, is exempt. That said, an informal list of guidelines for interacting with another hunter's dog might look as follows:

- *Ask the owner before the hunt about specific dos and don'ts.* Are you only going to shoot birds that are pointed? What about rabbits? I'm big on rabbits—absolutely love to eat them—and I'll shoot them every chance I get over my Labs; however, there are other hunters who would just as soon you don't. And there are those who would beat you down if you even mention the word *rabbit* around them and their dogs. What's the answer? Ask first.
- *Don't give commands to another hunter's dog.* He or she spends a lot of time working with that hound and really doesn't appreciate your confusing the critter with your "Do this and do that." Best to keep your mouth shut and your eyes open.
- *Don't try to take birds from a dog you don't know.* In twenty years, I've seen only one dog that growled and actually nipped at a nonowner trying to take a rooster away from him, a bird that was presented to the nonowner by the dog. Regardless, unless the owner says, "Sure, he'll deliver 'em to anyone; just take 'em," let the owner be the one who gets the bird.

- *Don't give the dog food or treats without first checking with the owner.* Sure, I love to give a hardworking hound half a MoonPie, but there's a chance that Rover has a special diet, sugar issues, or any of a thousand other problems that make a MoonPie a really bad idea. If the owner says it's fine, go ahead; if not, don't do it.

- *Never physically reprimand another hunter's dog.* This includes swatting, kicking, smacking . . . anything. Sure, my Labs aren't 100 percent all the time, and there are times when I'll swat them on the butt to drive home the point that whatever they did immediately preceding the swat was bad; however, I don't want to see you smack my dog. If I do and your name isn't Mrs. Julia Johnson, there's a good chance we'll have issues. I'm sure other hunters feel the same way about their dogs.

- *Always be cognizant of the other hunter's dog.* Watch what the dog does. Listen to what the owner says. Maybe it's a high-strung spaniel that jumps at the flush and follows the tail feathers into the air . . . whatever. If you pay 100 percent attention while you're hunting over your dog, give the other man's hound 150 percent.

Dogs come and go through the cover constantly. It's your job—your responsibility—to know where they are before you take the safety off.

Lee Harstad's yellow Lab, Maggie, performs equally well on waterfowl and upland birds—
a definite plus for those seeking a versatile utility hound.

A springer spaniel might be just the dog you're looking for. If you're like me, though, and hunt everything with feathers, then—surprise!—I'd definitely recommend a Labrador retriever. With a Lab, you have the tool to hunt mallards along an ice-choked river, mourners during the heat of mid-September, and roosters at the end of October, all out of the same package. Miss the point, you say? No, what you're talking about is the absence of a point—a quivering canine figure locked solidly in time, olfactory senses on red alert. Well, sir, there are indeed pointing Labs; in fact, my Jet is a pointing Lab. Any other questions?

Kids and/or Other Dogs

Do you have children? Do children often visit? Is there already a pheasant dog in the family? These, too, are factors when it comes time to whether to get a dog and what breed. Some pointers have an attitude around other dogs. Two males, regardless of lineage, may have territorial issues. Females also can get cranky around other dogs. My Jet has the capability to get her hindquarters in a bunch in the presence of other canines, if I'm not watching the situation closely—and she's a sweetheart. There's just that chance.

And with kids? Any dog can be fantastic and any dog can be problematic to some degree. Labs and golden retrievers both are wonderful around children; however, their size and frequent enthusiasm can be tough on the little ones. Even the smaller spaniels can bounce a toddler onto his or her back in the blink of an eye. It comes down, simply, to keeping an eye on things. Jealousy can pose a problem should the dog be there first and an infant come along after the fact. "What's that tiny squirming, squalling human doing here?"—that kind of thing. Some breeds are tolerant; some, such as cocker spaniels, are less so. My advice? Introduce the newest addition to the family, Rover included, with care, caution, and a very close eye.

*There's absolutely nothing that says a hunting dog can't be a pet
or a people dog. Most, fortunately, are.*

*Tell me . . . does it look like Deacon (front) and his mother, Jet, have more energy
at this stage of the game than I do? You bet they do!*

TRAINING TOOLS AND RESOURCES

Multitudinous books have been written on the subject of training hunting dogs. And because of the wealth of information that's available elsewhere, I'm not going to spend much time on it here although—and I have been told I possess an aversion to brevity—I will say a few things on the matter.

1. You cannot force desire or a willingness to hunt onto a dog, no matter how hard you try or how badly you want to. A dog can be forced to retrieve. It can be forced off the couch. It can be forced to sit, come, stay, lie down, and on and on and on . . . but it cannot have desire or natural ability forced upon it. Why do I mention this? If what you're doing is trying to mold a pheasant

dog, then you should start with the ingredients necessary for a good pheasant dog—namely, a talented mama and daddy. Sure, you can end up with a wonderful hound, courtesy of no-paper, no-hunting background parents—just come and look at Maggie if you want living, breathing, though soon to be retired proof of that. If you want to play the odds, however, start with a good bloodline (though the dog doesn't necessarily have to come from papered stock) and go from there.

2. Anyone, and I mean anyone, can teach any dog the basic commands, such as come, sit, and stay. And that's where you start, with the basics. First, however, you as the human instructor need to learn the basics, if you don't know them already,

*Training never stops. Here, my Pop and I work and play
with nine-month-old Deacon.*

before you're qualified to pass them along to your
new canine companion. What are the basic commands and how do you teach them? Buy a book
like Kevin Michalowski's *15 Minutes to a Great
Dog* or Richard Wolter's *Gun Dog,* an incredible
hardcover book that can also be used as a training
tool, particularly if you now own a Labrador
retriever. Read it and use it. Have one of the
employees at the local Petco, PetSmart, Bass Pro,
Cabela's, or the like suggest either some reading
material or DVDs. Perhaps they can offer or know
of a local obedience course you might enroll your
new hunter in. Surf the Internet. Ask questions
at the nearby gun club. The bottom line is this: If
you're willing to devote the time and energy training your soon-to-be hunting dog, the resources,

particularly for the novice, are out there. All you
have to do is search.

3. One of the premier dog-training rules is to have
patience. If you don't have it, learn it. Good hunting
dogs aren't created, nor are they trained overnight.
Or over a weekend. Training takes time; it's just
that simple. Don't expect miracles if you're not willing to sacrifice.

4. If you ask Phil Bourjaily what it takes to train a
good hunting dog, he'll tell you without hesitation:
"Get the dog into birds. Lots of birds. And get
into lots of birds often." Thing is, and as elemental
as it sounds, Phil's right. Dogs are all about desire
and repetition. If your new English setter encounters roosters one weekend in October and two
weekends in November—and that's it—well, don't

Electronic collars are a personal choice. I don't use them; many people do. Understand that a collar isn't magic— training still has to have the human touch.

expect much unless it's a member of Mensa. On the other hand, an inexperienced or even mediocre dog has the potential to become a much better hunter, if you give it the opportunity to perform and grow by putting birds in its face. Hunt your dog as much as possible during the season. Join a preserve or, at the very least, visit a preserve as often as your schedule and wallet allow. Buy a rooster or two, and work with your dog in the spring and summer after the preserves have closed. Every bird that dog encounters equates to a learning experience. Yes, that may not be a favorable experience, but it will be a learning experience. That said, learn and move on. But, as Bourjaily says, get your dog into lots of birds.

5. Remember that training never truly ends. Everything is a learning experience. If that new Lab or wirehair begins to falter on the basics, then go back to the basics. When Deacon hit the age of two— the "terrible twos," as they're rightly named—he suddenly developed a hearing problem, figuratively speaking. He was testing Julie and me to see if we really meant what we were saying. Well, several swats on the butt later and an ear pinch or two, plus a patented lip grab by Julie once or twice, and now his hearing is all better. Cruel? No, I don't think so; no more so than is a judiciously applied spanking. Time out? Wasn't going to work—not with a Lab. Will he go through it again? Probably, and when he does, we'll apply pressure and hope to bring him back into line again. Some dogs learn it once and never forget. Others—most in fact—need reminding and refreshing.

6. We've never used electronics—e-collars or shock collars—on any of our dogs. Granted, there have been times when I would have liked to have dropped Jet to her knees for things like running pheasants into the next section, but I blame myself for many of her faults. She's just doing what comes naturally. It was my job to correct or reverse those natural trends, and somewhere down the line, I dropped the proverbial ball—completely or in part. But electronic collars are not a magic bullet. They won't right everything that's wrong. They won't, by themselves, make a bad dog good or a good dog great. Electronics are a tool, just like a hammer is tool, and a carpenter can't build a house with a hammer alone. "If you're not careful," Kevin Michalowski told me when I asked about e-collars, "you can cause more harm than good with a collar. You can end up making your dog afraid of birds or afraid of you, neither of which is good. You simply can't hammer a dog with a collar and expect anything good to come of it." All that said, though, electronic collars can play an important role in the training process, if they're used correctly. And there's no reason they shouldn't be used correctly, what with all the information available on the Internet or from the manufacturers themselves. Call Innotek, Tri-Tronics, or another reputable company and ask to speak to someone in the know. Your dog will thank you for it.

The Canine Assistants

There was a time during the late 1970s—my formative outdoor years, to be precise—when my father and I didn't use a dog for pheasants. We used beagles to hunt rabbits, and occasionally we'd have a hound that would speak up and get excited whenever she crossed paths with a rooster . . . however infrequently that was. It wasn't until much later in life, around 1994 if I remember correctly, that I actually starting hunting ringnecks and a variety of other gamebirds and waterfowl with the assistance of a procession of black Labrador retrievers. Today the thought of leaving the house for the uplands without a black dog in tow is as foreign as leaving without a shotgun. Or bullets.

Pheasants and dogs just go together. Fact is, at least to me, hunting and dogs go together, but in few circles, waterfowlers aside, are canines as much a part of the overall outdoor experience as they are for pheasants and pheasant hunters. Pointing dogs, flushing dogs, beagles—hell, one fellow I talked with on a western Washington release site said that his pup, a tail-curled-over-the-back fluffy husky-looking critter, dearly loved to hunt anything, including pheasants. And my thought was, so what if it's not a traditional pheasant dog? As long as the dog gets the bird into the air and makes an attempt at finding it after the shot—actual retrieval being a bonus—who cares what it looks like? That said, there are some very traditional breeds out there chasing roosters around, including these ten.

English pointer: The English pointer is a favorite among upland hunters coast to coast and is used in the pursuit of a variety of gamebirds including ringnecks, grouse, quail, and woodcock. With Spanish roots, but a primarily English history, this pointer dates back to the mid-seventeenth century.

English setter: I've found English setters, like Phil Bourjaily's partner, Ike, to be wonderfully mannered, handsome, and quite skilled at finding even particularly sneaky roosters.

Brittany spaniel: Our only pointing spaniel, the Brittany made its way to America in the 1930s. To call a Brittany energetic would be understatement at its finest; however, this breed's energy and enthusiasm often pay off in spades when the snow gets deep, the cover gets thick, and the roosters simply don't want to play fair . . . which they seldom do.

German shorthaired pointer: As was the case with many Germanic breeds, the German shorthaired pointer was originally bred as an all-around hunter, with a focus on European hares and deer. Recently, though, it has grown in popularity among the nation's pheasant hunters. Records trace the breed back to the fatherland during the latter portion of the 1800s; however, it wasn't until well after the turn of the century that this dog was seen in the States.

(continued on page 103)

A pointer working it well in the Nebraska Sandhills.

Above: A gentleman's English setter delivers a rooster to hand in the Sandhills Country of northcentral Nebraska.

Above right: Wisconsin's Paul Smith, aka Badger Man, with a cute little Brittany spaniel—as friendly and as hard-working a pup as you'll encounter.

Left: Riding in the back of the truck with the guys, ears flopping in the breeze. Ah, what I'd give for a dog's life.

Lab or Brittany, the breed doesn't matter. What matters is that you and your hound enjoy yourselves.

Vizsla: A ruggedly handsome dog, in my opinion, and a breed that is becoming more and more common, particularly, it seems, in the midwestern and eastern parts of the United States, the Vizsla—and it's pronounced *VEES-lah*—is also a shorthaired pointer, though of Hungarian descent.

Weimaraner: Another German, the weimaraner also was bred as a big-game hunter; however, with the lack of roe deer in the United States, uplanders soon found something other for the Deutsch dog to chase.

German wirehaired pointer: Introduced to America around 1920, the German wirehaired pointer is a multitasker; that is, the breed sees duty as a pointer, a water retriever, and an accomplished fetcher of rabbits and hares.

Labrador retriever: Every houndsman will, at some point in his life, have something good to say about his dog, regardless of its lineage. I'm no different—I love Labs! They're extremely intelligent, very enthusiastic, incredible hunters. Water doesn't faze them, nor do harsh temperatures, deep snow, or ridiculously thick cover. They also make excellent family pets; however, be warned that those tails can and will clear a coffee table quicker than you can blink . . . so there's that. The first recorded birth of a Labrador in a color other than black was a yellow pup born in 1899. Today three flavors exist—black, yellow, and chocolate. *(continued on page 105)*

Left: "Okay, Dad! We got one, but there's more out there!"
SOUTH DAKOTA TOURISM

Above: David Draper's pup, Dublin, isn't getting too far away from the vehicle he trusts is going to get him into the field and into those old rooster pheasants.

Below: He's old and he's tired, but damn, did he find his share of roosters. He deserves a break.

Run, run, run, run . . . then sleep. It's a puppy's life, but he'll be chasing cockbirds soon enough.

Golden retriever: Developed in the late nineteenth century, golden retrievers—or simply, goldens—are today recognized as one of the world's most versatile breeds. As well as working for their hunter companions, goldens often are chosen to work as guide or support dogs for the blind or physically challenged and are commonly seen serving with the nation's search-and-rescue teams. What's more, the dogs are tremendously friendly, fiercely loyal, and right dandy pheasant chasers.

English springer spaniel: As is the case with the Brittany, the springer spaniel and the phrase "a bundle of energy" are synonymous. Still, it's an excellent choice for the pheasant hunter, though a little high-strung for some.

CHAPTER 6

A Wild Alternative: Preserves

"I CAUGHT THIS ONE HERE. YOU WANT I SHOULD throw it up in the air and then you shoot it?" Unimpressed, I shook my head and went back to the clubhouse, where I had a most interesting discussion with the owner of the facility and went on my way—$35 poorer, but millions upon millions of dollars wiser.

Oh, the rooster jumped all right, but not until I was twenty feet past him and looking in the opposite direction. Rocket-propelled from the get-go, the cockbird screamed away, cackling with every wingbeat. My first attempt to stop him was just that, an attempt, and a futile attempt, to be absolutely correct. My second? Well, that one, as my father was always fond of saying, could just as effectively have been thrown right straight up in the air. "Wow," said my sarcastic host. "You'd never know he was raised indoors and exercised in a flight pen. Pretty slow, aren't they?" And with that, he turned away, but not before cracking a smile so wide I feared he would rupture his face.

With the two stories above, I'm well on my way to discussing shooting preserves. But before I go any further with this discussion, let me preface this section with this comment: As is the case with damn near anything—cars, hotel rooms, computer equipment . . . hell, for that matter, marriage partners—

Done correctly, preserves can offer up a pheasant hunting experience impossible to tell from the wild. SOUTH DAKOTA TOURISM

Mike Miller, owner of K & M Hunting in Plankinton, South Dakota, shares a laugh with Allison Thompson of Mitchell prior to a hunt getting under way.

there are good shooting preserves and there are bad shooting preserves.

But what makes one shooting preserve *good* and another *bad*? Before getting into the pros and cons, let's first take a look at shooting preserves. A shooting preserve, at least by my definition, is a state-licensed, intensely managed piece of property, the size of which can vary from one hundred acres to ten thousand acres, give or take, on which hunting is offered and conducted as a business. Shooting preserves, sometimes referred to as hunting preserves, often offer a long list of hunting opportunities—several different types of upland birds, waterfowl, big game, and wild turkeys, to name just a handful—but we're going to concern ourselves here strictly with hunting ring-necked pheasants.

Think of a shooting preserve as the hunting equivalent of an à la carte restaurant. On most preserves, you

In many cases, the gunning opportunities are considerably more plentiful on well-run shooting preserves than they are in the wild. SOUTH DAKOTA TOURISM

address the owner and order off a menu. "I'd like a dozen roosters released," you say. "That will be $17.50 per bird," says the owner. You pay the price, the birds are liberated, and you conduct your hunt. When the hunt concludes, you tip your guide, who often doubles as your dog handler unless you use your own dog; pick up your processed birds, which have been cleaned for a nominal fee; and go home to relive the memories.

Certainly, there often is more to it than this. On preserves in some states, such as Iowa and South Dakota, wild birds are hunted right along with the released birds, adding an air of authenticity to the experience. Hunters often have the opportunity to use their own dogs, if they wish. A good shooting preserve will approximate, if not duplicate, the natural cover found in the immediate area. The pheasants, too, should be near mirror images of the real thing: strong fliers, good looking with fully feathered tails, not bedraggled, and capable of frustrating man and beast alike, just like their wild counterparts. Ideally, when it's all said and done, the owner of the preserve would love to hear these words: "I couldn't tell the difference." That, in a nutshell, is the essence of preserve pheasant hunting, the re-creation of a 100 percent wild, natural outdoor experience under controlled circumstances. Think it's easy? You've never owned a preserve.

For now, though, what you need to know is that a shooting preserve is a place where pheasants are hunted for a fee. So, it then becomes quite understandable to ask, why would anyone, particularly those living in rooster-rich states such as South Dakota and Kansas, patronize such a pay-to-play hunting facility? Truthfully, the reasons are many:

Preserves offer tremendous outdoor learning environments for both experienced and inexperienced alike.

- *No permission and no public-ground crowds:* On a shooting preserve, all you really need is a wallet and the desire to enjoy yourself. You don't need to request landowner permission, and there are no crowded parking lots and orange-clad hordes as are common on many of the nation's public lands.
- *Longer seasons:* A typical shooting preserve opens on September 1 and closes on April 1 of the following year; some are open and provide pheasant hunting opportunities year-round. Compared with even a liberal state season on wild birds, such as Iowa's seventy-three-day pheasant season in 2004–05,

these shooting preserves offer hunting far beyond what most folks would normally have available. In essence, there's very little downtime on a shooting preserve, sometimes none.
- *Liberal bag limits:* On many shooting preserves, the daily bag limit, to use the term loosely, is dictated only by what you want to spend. "Each bird costs XX dollars," says the man in charge, and you plan your day accordingly.
- *Controlled conditions:* Generally speaking, the shooting preserve experience is relatively controlled, particularly from a safety standpoint. Certainly, accidents can happen; however, the fact that most preserve outings are overseen by a nonhunting employee whose primary function is to ensure the safety of

*Everything considered, today's shooting preserves—with exceptions,
certainly—are very reasonably priced across the board.*

all of the participants helps minimize the chance
of anything going awry. In keeping with this notion
of controlled conditions, many shooting preserves
groom their cover to make it accessible to all hunters,
even in some cases the physically challenged. No
eight-foot-high switchgrass here, though I have
on some occasions found myself pushing standing
corn toward blockers while on a preserve hunt. It
all depends.

- *Excellent learning and training experience:* Shooting
preserves can be excellent learning and training
facilities for new or young hunters and up-and-
coming canines. Think of it this way: A new pilot
doesn't immediately solo first rattle out of the box,
now does he? Of course not. He spends time with
the manual, then he spends time with an instructor
who takes him into the field and presents him with
real-life situations. Finally, once the new pilot has
some type of flying foundation on which to build,
he does his solo flight. Shooting preserves can
often provide a similar scenario for new hunters or
young dogs, serving as an exemplary classroom in
which to learn. There's no question that the birds
will be present, and each individual encounter by
the pupil, be it an adult, child, or dog, can be carefully monitored. Birds can be presented time and
time again. Most agree that as a training tool,
shooting preserves are invaluable.

- *Reasonably priced:* In the grand scheme of things,
shooting preserves are actually quite reasonably
priced. Hell, you can easily spend $12 on a large,
three-topping pizza and a two-liter bottle of Pepsi
. . . unless you have it delivered, and then dinner,
with tip, can cost you $20 or more. Isn't a $15 rooster pheasant, then, a pretty good deal? When you
consider the price of a so-called "free hunt," with
cost of fuel, license, time to find property, obtaining
landowner permission, and perhaps a lease, three
or four cockbirds courtesy of the local shooting
preserve starts to sound more and more like a fine
idea. Still, with preserve hunting, like much in
modern society, you get what you pay for. Some
preserves offer a long list of options and prices
where the sky is the proverbial limit. Later, we'll
look at the question of price and what you might
want to ask the preserve owner when planning your
outing. For the present, let's just say that preserves
can be a good deal.

In addition to pheasants, chukars (red-legged partridge) are one of several gamebirds available on many of the nation's shooting preserves. Bobwhites and flighted mallards are also popular.

Above: Outdoor magazines and other publications can provide excellent information regarding shooting preserves from coast to coast.
Right: Ah, yes, and then there's the meals, one of my favorite aspects of the modern shooting preserve.

- *Additional sporting opportunities:* You want to hunt chukar or bobwhites or flighted mallards along with your pheasants? Some preserves have them, and it's just a matter of quick-drawing your wallet and letting the owner know of your wishes. How about a round of sporting clays or an hour on the trap range before hitting the field? Many privately owned facilities offer their clients full use of sporting clays, trap, or skeet ranges right there on the property as sort of a warm-up to the main event—for a little extra folding money, in most cases. Some outfitters provide two distinctly different outdoor activities during a single day's booking. For example, Steve Fahey and Cherokee Charters arranges for you to hunt birds in the morning and fish South Dakota's Lake Sharpe for walleyes and white bass in the afternoon. The shooting preserve experience can be a complete outdoor experience; it just depends on how much time you have, how much money you want to spend, and what you want to do.
- *Noteworthy room and board:* Let me say this without hesitation: Regardless of the quality of the

preserve hunting experience—and trust me, I've had it from good to flat-out poor and everything in between—the food, be it breakfast, lunch, or dinner, has, without fail, been excellent. It hasn't always been fancy, and I'd just as soon it's not, but there's always been plenty of it and it's always been tasty. As with a soldier, a hunter's motivation in large part depends on food consumption, and it's been my experience—and my waistline stands as testimony—that shooting preserves and good food go hand in hand. Or hand to mouth, whichever the case may be. As for rooms . . . well, let me just say this. After walking all day, a bed becomes a bed, regardless of the price tag attached, and I've never slept in a poor room following a satisfying day afield. 'Nough said.

WHERE TO FIND A PRESERVE

If you're new to this shooting preserve thing, your first question is also the most understandable: Where do I begin looking? Fortunately, the preserve hunter's research or reference tools are many and include the following:

- *Black's Wing & Clay Handbook:* If you do anything at all with a shotgun, you're missing out tremendously if you don't have a copy of *Black's Wing & Clay Handbook.* This five hundred-plus-page handbook contains information on everything shotgun, from shooting schools to reloading equipment to, yes, a state-by-state listing of shooting preserves with such information as telephone numbers, addresses, websites, what birds are available, any additional shooting opportunities offered on the facility, and much, much more. Believe me when I say that the book is as indispensable a reference source as a reloading manual is to the man seated in front of the MEC 600 Junior. Currently, the handbook is published by the Ehlert Publishing Group, with copies available by writing Black's Sporting Directories, 6420 Sycamore Lane N. #100, Maple Grove, MN 55369, or by calling 800-848-6247.
- *State fish & wildlife agencies:* Because shooting preserves are licensed by the state fish and wildlife agency, it then makes sense that the state fish and wildlife agency would have a list of those preserves, eh? Well, a lot of the departments do, but some, for whatever reason, don't make those available to the general public. I don't know why. Still, lacking a current copy of the aforementioned *Black's Wing & Clay Handbook,* your first telephone call should be to your state fish and wildlife agency and, once connected, simply ask, "Do you have a list of shooting preserves? You don't? Well, where can I find one?"
- *State tourism departments:* Sometimes the state fish and wildlife folks will pass you off to the public information section of the state tourism department . . . and this isn't necessarily a bad thing. Almost without exception, state tourism personnel are an incredibly helpful bunch, and most will go out of their way to make sure you get the information you need, and then some. For instance, if you were to call Eileen at the South Dakota Department of Tourism and State Development, she'll likely pass you along to the agency's media relations program chieftain, who will help you find a preserve. Chances are good that it's one he has personally hunted, and he can tell you things you won't find in any reference book or on the Internet.

- *Outdoor publications:* Most hunting publications, big and small, include advertisements and listings for local, state, and regional shooting preserves. Here, you might want to think of doing a couple different things. Certainly, you can use the contact information contained in the ad to call the preserve yourself. Or, as I've been known to do, you can call the publication and ask to speak to the ad representative who deals directly with Ma & Pa Kettle's Shooting Club. This accomplishes two things. First, it lets both the ad rep *and* the shooting preserve owner who placed the ad know that it is indeed working. Second, and more significant to you as a prospective client of Ma & Pa's Shooting Club, it affords you the opportunity to get some insider information about the place.
- *The Internet:* And finally, there's the Internet. Yes, the World Wide Web can be a great source of information, and yes, it can be a tremendously valuable research tool when it comes time to do your homework concerning a specific shooting preserve . . . or locating a preserve in the first place; *however,* I caution you with these words: Do not go on the say-so of the Internet alone. You need to take what's being said about any particular facility with a grain of salt until such a time as you can prove or disprove it. How do you do that? Talk, electronically if need be, to several different people on a discussion forum or website about your preserve of choice. Then ask the preserve for references. Cross-check the forums with the references and come up with your own conclusion. It takes a little time, but when you're looking at spending money on a shooting preserve experience, what's a little time?

IDENTIFYING A *GOOD* PRESERVE

What, then, constitutes the difference between a *good* preserve and a *bad* preserve? Anyone who's hunted more than one shooting preserve is going to have a good story and a bad story. Ask the person who's hunted one hundred such places, and they're going to have tales of excellence as well as horror stories. The bottom line is that preserves are no different from any other consumer item. You get what you pay for, and if you don't do your homework before the purchase and you get stung . . . well, that's technically known as a "shame on you."

A post-hunt roundtable in South Dakota comes to the conclusion that the morning was a success, thanks to a conscientious and hard-working preserve owner and operator.

So is there a way to keep from getting stung and having a bad experience? First of all, get it out of your head that there's anything wrong with asking questions of your prospective business partner—the guy or gal who owns the shooting preserve that you're looking to patronize. Truth is, if I were a preserve owner, I'd be more surprised by—and cautious of—those who *didn't* ask questions before coming out than uncomfortable and irritated at those who did. With that said, what questions actually need asking? Though each preserve may warrant its own individualized series of questions, these should get you started regardless of where you're hunting:

- *Will I need a license?* For a fee, state-licensed preserves will supply you with their own preserve license. This paperwork is good on the preserve only and is typically the only type of license paperwork necessary; however, you'll want to make sure of this.

- *What will I pay?* This should go without saying, but get the prices up front. Do you pay for a certain number of birds to be released, or do you pay by the bird for each bird harvested? Different facilities handle this in different ways. Are gratuities to dog handlers, bird processors, and the like included, or are these paid separately? What does the preserve license cost? Are there bird-processing fees? What about meals or a room, if you'll be using their facilities? It's no different from buying a new pickup truck—ask about the options and what each will cost.

- *What about my hunting dog?* Can I bring my own dog and run my own dog my way? If I bring my own dog for more than a day hunt, do they have kennel facilities and are they included in the overall cost of the outing? Most preserves offer trained dogs and experienced handlers, so don't feel at a disadvantage if you're not among the canine-owning crowd. Ask if said dog and handler are included in the fee.

- *How would you describe a typical day's hunt?* What can you expect during a day on the shooting preserve? Will a full day include a morning and afternoon hunt along with breakfast and lunch? How long do the hunts—the actual field time—typically last? Can you pay for just a morning or an afternoon outing if that's all you want?

Typically, licenses are available at the preserve. However, this is certainly a question worth asking prior to your trip.

- *How is the cover and how are the birds?* It's worth quite a bit to not be surprised when hunt day arrives and you're standing at the edge of the first covert. What does the preserve's cover look like? Do the birds look good and fly well? After the proprietor gives you some answers, jump right in with the following question.

- *Do you have a website, brochure, or video?* In this modern electronic age, there's no reason to book a hunt on a shooting preserve based on a telephone conversation alone. Take your research to the next level and get a look at the preserve *before* you go. Asking for a brochure to review is a good idea. A brochure can reveal much about a shooting preserve through photographs, descriptive text, and testimonials from past clients. But brochures can only take you so far. Internet websites can raise the informational bar quite a bit, but best is a video or DVD of the facilities and a hunt in progress, and many preserves will be more than glad to drop one in the mail for your review.

This group in northern Iowa discusses how the morning's hunt will unfold.

- *Do you provide guns and ammunition?* If you're looking at visiting a shooting preserve for the purpose of shooting, you probably own a shotgun. That's not always the case, however, and there may be instances, such as corporate outings that include novice hunters, where members of the hunting

The cover should look natural and provide a realistic backdrop or stage for your outing. If your prehunt homework shows otherwise, I'd suggest going elsewhere. SOUTH DAKOTA TOURISM

party may not own shotguns. Then the question "Do you have shotguns to loan?" becomes a legitimate concern. As far as ammunition goes, chances are you've supplied yourself with pheasant bullets prior to the hunt. I did hunt on one preserve in South Dakota where the owner was adamant about his clients using quality ammunition. "No sense in paying good money and coming all this way if you're going to use those cheap shells," he told the group at the close of his prehunt safety discussion. "If you've got those cheapie things, I've got good ammunition I'll sell you," he continued, leaving no room—absolutely none—for discussion. Not surprisingly, he made several sales that morning. Lesson learned? Take quality ammunition. The preserve owner might require it, and those roosters certainly are owed that respect.

- *Do you offer lodging, food, and other amenities?* In keeping with the notion of the à la carte menu,

most preserves offer their clients some type of package, such as a half-day hunt with lunch, a full-day hunt with breakfast and lunch, or a two- or three-day trip with three squares a day and a pillow on which to lay your head at the end of each hunt. All you and your wallet have to do is decide what you would like and can afford, and then ask, "How much will this room and board cost?"

- *What's your procedure for game processing?* Does the facility offer bird cleaning, and if so, is it included in the total price? If not, what is the price per bird? I enjoy cleaning and would rather prepare my own roosters, and thus I will often ask the owner whether he minds if I clean my own birds and if he has a bird-processing shed where I might do the work. Trust me . . . after he's cleaned two thousand roosters, the owner or head guide is not about to say no when I ask if I can clean my own birds.

Though most gunners will bring their own shotgun fodder, the query "Do you have ammunition for sale on-site?" is not out of line when researching a new facility.

In fact, a secure man will probably hug you just for asking, but it's okay. He's just happy.

• *How are bagged birds transported?* Whether you're leaving the fictional Pin Oak Ridge Hunt Club and Shooting Preserve with three roosters or thirty, I can guarantee you that each of those pheasants will be wearing jewelry on one leg or the other. Issued by the same state fish and wildlife agency that licensed the facility, these so-called preserve tags, small numbered bands of aluminum or tough plastic, allow law enforcement personnel to differentiate between wild birds, for which there is a state-imposed bag limit, and preserve birds, for which typically there is none. Tagging birds harvested on a licensed preserve is, in my opinion, a given; however, it certainly can't hurt to ask about the process of transporting birds from the facility to your place of residence. And while you're at it, ask the owner how he or she handles the same-day transportation of birds. Most preserves keep an ample supply of cleaned, frozen, and packaged pheasants on hand for their clients. At hunt's end, the freshly bagged birds are simply traded for an equal number of previously packaged ones, and you're on your way. It's the typical scenario, but ask.

• *How about hunters with disabilities?* "We have one of those Arctic Cat six-wheelers," said Steve Hanning, a partner in eastern Washington's Outdoor Hunting Adventures and Miller Ranch, "and we'll put a fellow in the back of one of those. Once the dog goes on point, we'll back that around, flush the bird, and the hunter will have an opportunity. We've done that a couple times." And I'm sure that across the country, similar opportunities for disabled outdoorsmen and women to enjoy an afternoon afield chasing roosters exist aplenty, but you need to ask. Can the preserve cater to a hunter with limited mobility?

The Preserve as Classroom and Opportunity

Hunting offers no guarantees, which is probably why Webster's defines the word hunt as "to try to find; to search or to seek." To try to find, at least in my way of thinking, implies that though you might find what you're looking for, you might not—thus, the "no guarantee" aspect of hunting.

Preserve hunting, on the other hand, comes with the implication that you are indeed going to find what you're looking for. Here, it's pheasants. You don't go to the grocery store on the off chance of finding a sirloin or a box of Pop-Tarts, do you? Likewise, folks don't go to a preserve with the thought that they can spend their money and maybe, just maybe, see a pheasant.

It is, then, this *guarantee* element of hunting preserves that makes them the ideal choice for outdoor educators, experienced hunters, looking for a classroom setting in which their students, new or inexperienced hunters, can and will be exposed to those events that lead to learning. What the hell am I talking about? It's like this. You don't take a five-year-old who's never fished before to Lake Saint Clair trolling for muskies and expect him to have the time of his life, do you? No, you take him to Farmer Brown's pond, which is full of stunted bluegills, and you spend the afternoon baiting and unhooking and baiting and unhooking while he catches fish after fish after fish—and giggles. The hunting preserve is to the new hunter what the farm pond is to the five-year-old.

What's the bottom line? The new hunter, whether aged eleven or thirty-one, wants to succeed, and success here is measured by actually seeing something at which to shoot and then shooting it. Preserves guarantee this, and in doing so—at least in my humble opinion—help foster interest and enthusiasm within this inexperienced individual.

Along with offering this so-called guaranteed experience, shooting preserves also provide as controlled a setting as you'll find in upland gunning—something like father and son sitting side by side squirrel hunting, only with roosters. "That's a rooster," says the teacher. "And that's a hen." "Are you ready?" More lessons. "Do you know where the dog is?" "Do you know where all your hunting partners are?" "Is it safe to shoot in that direction?" These situations and a whole lot more can be presented, thanks to the shooting preserve, and in the course of a single afternoon.

Opportunity, too, is a by-product of the shooting preserve. What do I mean by opportunity? Certainly, opportunity here can be defined as an experienced hunter's chance to harvest birds he or she otherwise wouldn't have seen, let alone bagged, as well as the educational opportunities. But what about opportunities for those with limited mobility? This might mean your seventy-five- or eighty-year-old father or grandfather, a lifelong pheasant hunter who just can't get around like he used to these days. Or it can mean a guy like our friend Eric McClenathan who, because of neurological issues, is more or less confined—though I use the word loosely, because there's not a thing that confines Eric—to a wheelchair. Most shooting preserves take such hunters into consideration, and tailor portions of their facility and sections of their acreage to those with mobility issues. Maybe your grandpa is transported along a route in a six-wheeled John Deere Gator, stopping periodically to walk into a point. Or perhaps there is a paved or groomed path that will safely accommodate Eric's wheelchair as he goes from point to point. Some facilities are already accessible; others are en route to becoming so. Regardless, they do exist and you can find them . . . and trust me, your grandpa and Eric McClenathan will thank you for having done so.

Preserves are excellent places to introduce young hunters to the joys of the field. PHIL BOURJAILY

*Above: The "war wagon"—otherwise known as
transportation into and out of the field. Does
your prospective shooting preserve provide
such transportation?*
*Left: Talking with past clients is probably the most
reliable method of getting a good, in-depth look at
a shooting preserve's day-to-day operation.*

Can they work with folks in wheelchairs? Is it possible for a handicapped shooter to sit, with a partner, as a blocker and shoot driven birds? I've had the pleasure of working with a couple different avid outdoorsmen confined to wheelchairs, and both enjoyed themselves tremendously sitting at the end of a milo field and pass-shooting roosters—all possible, thanks to the shooting preserve.

- *What about sporting clays, trap, or skeet?* Some folks go to a shooting preserve explicitly for the purpose of hunting pheasants. And that's fine; however, often other shotgunning opportunities can be had while visiting the facility. Today a sporting-clays course, along with either a formal or informal trap or skeet range, is standard fare on many shooting preserves. Each can provide you with the chance for a warm-up before hitting the field or a leisurely

way to relax after a morning's hunt, but you need to know whether such facilities exist before you can plan your little friendly competitive trap shoot—so ask.

- *Do you have references from past clients?* Don't underestimate the importance of asking for references from past clients. Have any magazine or newspaper articles been written about the facility that you might review? Any television shows or videos filmed? It's been my experience that all good shooting preserves maintain an up-to-date list of references and will make that list available— often offering even before they're asked to provide such information. If, by some chance, a facility does not have a reference list or balks at the query "May I have a list of past clients?"—I'd start looking elsewhere.

CHAPTER 7

From Field to Feast

LET ME START BY SAYING THAT I'VE NEVER tasted a bad pheasant. Honestly. Some have been a little better than others—a little more tender, a little more moist, a little more flavorful; however, I've never had a bad one. Maybe I've just been lucky. Or maybe, just maybe, you have to work really, really hard to make a pheasant taste bad. Oh, yes, I'm sure it could be done, but the fact remains—I haven't had one.

So now that I have you all arguing amongst yourselves, reminiscing about the last boot-leather rooster you had the misfortune of being seated behind, let me take this one step further and say this: Pheasant is chicken. Not in the sense you're thinking, although I'm sure that even the wildest rooster can be made to resemble old Foghorn Leghorn in a culinary sense, what with a sauce here, a spice there, and a little bit of good, old-fashioned chicken stock thrown in for good measure. Truth is that if you tried, damn near anything could be made to taste like chicken.

But that's not what I'm talking about here. What I'm referring to when I make this comparison between rooster and Rhode Island Red is that like chicken, pheasant lends itself—and well, I might add—to a lengthy, if not infinite, list of recipes and cooking methods. I'm no Iron Chef, mind you, but I'd like to think I can still find my way around a kitchen or a barbecue; that said, even I have put together a pheasant-based résumé that includes smoked, baked, fried, deep-fried,

It all starts here. Will the rooster taste good, or will he taste bad? What happens now determines everything.

Dutch ovened, grilled, jerkied, sautéed, stir-fried, broiled, roasted, stuffed and roasted, and kabobbed . . . and I'm not even sure if *kabobbed* is a word, but I've done it with pheasant. Birds in my kitchen have been dipped in egg, rolled in flour, filled with apples, browned in olive oil, soaked in marinades, and drizzled with a combination of orange juice and Two Fingers tequila. No, wait. I was drizzled with the Two Fingers and OJ, and inadvertently the rooster got a dose, too.

My point here isn't about tequila, but rather this: Pheasants are excellent on the table. They're wonderful as experimental dishes. They can be prepared with little or nothing in terms of ingredients. And what about your kitchen and the appliances, aka gadgets, necessary to cook a rooster to perfection? Well, sir, they've been done in everything from $200 Farberware roasters to trail-worn cast-iron skillets older than dirt itself. And you know what? Chances are if you tried 'em both, you'd never be able to tell the difference. No, sir. Pheasants are just plain, good food.

But before you get to thinking that the instructions for pheasant under glass read something like "Step 1, shoot. Step 2, enjoy," there are a handful of intermediate steps that occur between the bird in the bag and the one on the table that you should be aware of.

FIELD CARE

Those of you who have read my other books will recall me saying this at least once before, but it's worth saying again (and again and again): A good wild-game dinner actually begins in the field. Translation? If you give the roosters you bring to bag the same care and attention you would give, say, a worn-out, bald tire then why should you expect those birds to taste any better than that worthless circle of rubber? A truckload of cranberries and an ocean of marinade aren't going to make a bad pheasant taste better. Certainly, both cranberries and marinade can help hide the fact that you left your limit of cockbirds lying, breast down and in the direct sun, in the back of your pickup for the better

A fine fat, corn-fed Iowa rooster—and a young one at that. This one should be excellent on the table.

Left: A bird strap like the one Richard Creason uses here allows birds to cool quickly—a definite plus when it comes to flavor enhancers.
Below: Matching your firearm and your ammunition to the game being hunted is the first step to procuring high-quality foodstuffs.

part of the afternoon, but good eats? I don't think so. The trick here, folks, is not to mask a bad taste during the cooking process, but to ensure via good field care and common sense that the bad taste doesn't have a chance to get started. And that begins in the field.

So with all that finger-shaking behind us, here's a list, then, of dos and don'ts for the field:

- *Don't overgun yourself.* More precisely, don't use ammunition—shot charges or shot sizes—more appropriate for shooting pterodactyls than for something that weighs in at two and a half pounds. Heavy loads, particularly at close range, can really do a number on a rooster, and it's tough to do anything appetizing with a Swiss-cheese pheasant. So use enough gun, but not too much.
- *Do get your birds cool as quickly as possible.* Shooting vests or coats with game bags are great for carrying birds, but they're not much in the way of air cir-

culation . . . and you want that air circulation, as it helps dissipate the residual body heat from the birds themselves. Here you might want to give some thought to using a mesh or otherwise open game bag or pouch, especially during the early season or when temperatures are above, say, 50 degrees F. You can also use a bird tote or strap attached to your belt. True, the birds are exposed to the air and thus cool quickly; however, I'm not much on a brace of big, old Iowa roosters slapping against my leg with every step. Not to mention the fact that they catch on everything I walk through and at the end of half a day look like colorful feather pillows that have caught the better part of a belt of 7.62 M-60 rounds.
- *Don't pile your birds in the back of your pickup in the sun.* Would you take a five-pound porterhouse and slap it on the hood of your Dodge pickup for the afternoon? In Texas? In June? Enough said.

I know, I know. I staged this one—they're wild birds, by the way—to demonstrate what not *to do with your birds.*

• *Do gut your birds if the weather is extremely warm.* Truthfully, I seldom gut birds in the field. An open body cavity is just an invitation to have your rooster prestuffed with such things as cockleburs, beggar ticks, grasshoppers, and milkweed down; however, if the weather is extremely warm, such as during an April or September preserve hunt, I will sometimes take a minute—and that's all it takes—to make a quick slice alongside the vent and draw (gut) my birds as I kill them. If I think there's a chance of this happening, I'll pack a small Ziploc bag filled with folded paper towels into my vest pocket. As I gut each bird, I stuff a crumpled sheet or two of paper towel into the body cavity, my thinking being that this will prevent, or at least decrease the likelihood of bad things getting into my birds.

• *Do prepare yourself for a trip to the taxidermist.* Fill a Ziploc freezer bag with a dozen cotton balls, a flat resealable aluminum foil dispenser of wet wipes, and a pair of old knee-high nylon stockings and carry it in your game vest. Let's say you shoot a tremendous example of a rooster pheasant: long spurs, a twenty-eight-inch tail, high "ears" . . . the

whole nine yards. Immediately you decide—taxidermist! Quickly take out your Ziploc bag and use one of the wet wipes to gently remove any blood on the feathers. Then stuff a cotton ball in the bird's mouth to prevent any blood or other fluid from soiling the feathers in transit. Finally, slip your prize headfirst into one of the nylon stockings, which holds all the feathers in place until you get the bird home and quick-draw your checkbook . . . but that's another story.

SAFE TRANSPORTATION

Eventually you and your birds are going to leave the field. Next stop? Home, or the lodge or cabin or wherever it is you're staying throughout your pheasant hunt. Here, the plot, at least in terms of what you want to do with the pheasants you've bagged, thickens just a bit. Before we go on to the next step in the processing process, known as *the separation of fowl and feathers,* there are a few things to note.

First and second, you're going to want to ensure that your birds not only are kept cool while in transit, but also are somewhat protected from the elements, including the wind. If you know the temperatures are going to be higher than, say, 50 degrees on the day of your hunt, take an extra minute to throw a cooler in the back of your rig. A gallon milk jug filled with frozen water is all the chill you need. It beats the traditional bag of ice, which thaws, leaks, and turns your birds into a soggy, though admittedly cool, mess.

Protection? Now why protect something that by all accounts has ceased needing protection? By protection, I'm talking about carting your birds to the house or your place of lodging in a manner that they're not exposed to rain, buffeted by the wind, baked by the sun, or accessible to man or beast. True, I've never had a dog eat a pheasant, knock on wood, but I did have a beagle named Spike eat two bobwhite quail. Dug them out of the game bag of my old man's hunting vest, which itself was weighted by an eight-pack of POC, aka Pilsner on Call beer. That's right—ate 'em whole . . . beaks, feathers, feet, guts, everything. Imagine what an eighty-pound black Lab would do to a rooster if he were left alone with it while you went in for a posthunt pizza and a cold draft? I'm not saying it would happen, but why risk it?

You're also going to want to consider the legal aspects of transporting your birds from the field to their final resting place, whatever or wherever that might be. Rather than go into a lengthy, state-by-state explanation here, let me just say this: Read *and* understand the regulations regarding the transportation of legally harvested pheasants as they pertain to the state in which you're hunting. These rules, not surprisingly, can and often do differ from state to state. Some require a fully feathered wing to be left; others want the head. Still others want to see a wing *and* the head, whereas for some, a spurred leg is proof positive. What about processed birds? Again, read the regulations, but in most cases, processed birds destined for transport away from the place where they were harvested, be it an outfitter, lodge, or private land should include the fully feathered head.

Okay, so now you've gotten the birds home or to the facility where you're going to make them ready for either the table or the freezer. Now what? I've never hung pheasants—that is, treated them like waterfowl by gutting and hanging them, tail down, in a cool (40 degrees or cooler) place for a couple days to age. Some folks do, and by all means, that's fine. If done correctly—and by that I mean immediately gutting the birds, wiping the body cavity out, and then hanging them in a cool place—aging birds can do nothing but improve the flavor. With young roosters, this isn't nearly the issue that it might be with cocks that have survived a couple seasons. And so with that said, I'll leave the "to hang, or not to hang" verdict up to you.

One of my gunning partners is a firm believer in putting his birds, innards intact, into an outside refrigerator—"or hanging them outside," he says, "if it's not going to freeze them solid"—for a day or two, not so much to age but to firm up. He then dry-plucks his roosters, saying that the couple days in the fridge help prevent the skin from tearing during the cleaning process. Makes sense to me, and this eliminates the need to get your birds sopping wet from scalding . . . but we'll get to that in a minute. An exception to his "couple days in the fridge" method involves birds that were hard hit. Those he cleans immediately, he says, remembering a time or two when he waited and shouldn't have. Guess you can teach an old dog a new thing or two.

SEPARATION OF FOWL AND FEATHERS

At this point, the birds are at your processing station, which in my case consists of a workbench in the garage underneath a fluorescent twin-tube light. Everything I need is within reach. And so I'm standing there, looking down at a beautiful three-bird limit of wild Iowa roosters, thinking, "Okay, how do I want to do this?" How do you want to do this, this separation of feathers from fowl?

Truth is, every pheasant hunter has his or her favorite method for cleaning, aka processing, birds. Trying to get someone to change is like me trying to teach my father, a crappie fisherman for more than fifty years, a new and different way of filleting panfish. Oh, he watched and listened all right, but then he went right back to doing it the way he'd been doing it for fifty years.

That said, there are essentially four—I'll call them traditional—methods for cleaning pheasants: dry plucking, scalding, skinning, and filleting. Most, if not all, can be used in the processing of any upland gamebird. Some work better than others, where the word *work* can mean be more effective, be more expedient, or make for a more aesthetically pleasing end product,

to name just three definitions or dimensions. All
require surprisingly little in the way of equipment,
a good, heavy-spined knife being a denominator
common to all four. None of the methods I'll describe
are what I would call difficult; however, as with most
undertakings, your first attempts may be somewhat . . .
well, let's just say they might be a bit rough. Fear not,
for you'll improve.

Dry Plucking
Growing up, I never dry-plucked roosters. Why?
Because my old man didn't, that's why. Today, though,
I process probably a good half of the birds we get
annually with little more than time and a healthy set
of muscles between my thumb and forefinger. Translation: They get dry-plucked.

As is the case with all four of the cleaning methods, dry plucking has its pros and cons. True, it makes
for an excellent-looking final product, both on the
washboard and on the serving platter; however, unless
it's done carefully, dry plucking can result in the bird's
skin being torn, and you want that soon-to-be-golden-
brown skin left as intact as possible. And while we're
on the subject of skin—yes, dry plucking, unlike skinning or filleting, does preserve that moisture barrier,
skin, but it can be a time-consuming process. In fact,
dry plucking is probably the most time-consuming
method for separating a rooster from his feathers.
That, mind you, isn't necessarily a bad thing, but it
is certainly something to be considered.

Essentially, dry plucking is dry plucking—that
is, dry feathers are plucked from a dry pheasant. Dry
plucking can be done on either a fresh, warm rooster
or a chilled bird. With a warm bird, the cleaning job is
accomplished shortly after the hunt. That's a good thing,
but a warm rooster is also prone to skin tearing, which
damages the bird's best moisture-retention device.

One way around this plucking-and-tearing scenario
is to cool your birds before cleaning. If Mother Nature
pegs her thermometer between 35 and 40 degrees F,
by all means hang the birds out in the garage, shed . . .
somewhere they can chill but will be protected from
the elements, marauding cats, opossums, and the like.
If the temperature outside is above 40 degrees, put your
roosters in the fridge—twelve to twenty-four hours
ought to do the trick. What you're trying to accomplish
here is not to freeze the birds, but to chill both the skin

and any fat underneath. This sets, or firms, the skin and
does two good things. One, it makes feathers easier to
pluck, and two, it helps prevent tearing.

Now, let's say you're starting with a cold, ungutted
rooster, and you've decided to go the dry-plucking route.
Your list of equipment, then, consists of the following:

- *A suitably lighted work area.* It sounds elemental,
  I know, but it does help to have a work area with
  good lighting. As I was growing up, my father
  would put a cutting board, a square of three-
  quarter-inch plywood, on top of Mom's washing
  machine in the basement and cover the board with
  several sections of newspaper, thus creating a cleaning station à la Maytag. The washer was located next
  to the stainless-steel utility tubs with hot and cold
  running water, which made cleanup of both bird and
  bird hunter remarkably simple. And honestly? The
  entire process was incredibly self-contained, except
  for the occasional feather . . . or two . . . or many . . .
  that somehow escaped. Ma, she was an understanding woman.

- *A cutting board.* Take it from me and bitter experience: Do not gut or otherwise dismember pheasants on your mother's or wife's washing machine
  without using a cutting board. They won't think the
  etchings are nearly as cool as you do.

- *A bag-lined garbage can.* I find this the easiest way
  to work when I'm dry-plucking. I just pick the
  roosters, save the feathers I want to keep, toss the
  innards and the old newspaper I worked on into
  the bag, and put the bag out to be taken away with
  the next garbage pickup.

- *A stiff-spined knife.* You want a knife that falls
  somewhere between the flexibility of a fillet knife
  and the tree-chopping capabilities of a heavy-back-
  boned Rambo-esque piece of cutlery. For several
  years now, I've used a Buck Model 224 Ulti-Mate
  Stream knife with a 4.25-inch blade not only for all
  my upland-bird-cleaning duties, but for waterfowl
  as well. This particular knife was designed as a fisherman's piece, says Paul Gregg, marketing projects
  coordinator for Buck. "The handle is made of a
  material called Kraton, which is nonslip and actually gets tacky when it gets wet. The handle is also
  contoured and features finger grooves. The plastic
  sheath, you'll notice, has drain holes so that water

Left: My Pop plucks his birds after scalding them. I skin or fillet mine. It's all about what you wish to do with the final product.
Below: Pheasant-cleaning implements are elemental; however, a good sharp quality blade is essential.

won't collect in the sheath itself and start to work on the blade. We really put a lot of thought into the design of this knife." And he's right—they did put a lot of thought into it. Although I want to stop short of this being one of those damn advertorials, I would highly recommend this particular blade—or a model with similar features—to anyone looking for an excellent upland-bird-cleaning piece.

• *A supply of old newspaper.* What'd you think? Old newspaper isn't just for cleaning fish, you know.

Now before you get concerned that I've forgotten all about the Ziploc bags and the plastic wrap and the butcher paper and the vacuum packers—well, I haven't. First let's get the birds cleaned, then we'll talk about getting them into the deep freeze . . . if, that is, they're not going directly into the oven. But for right now, dry plucking:

STEP 1: A right-hander, I hold the rooster in my left hand by the legs, being careful of the spurs, and pick with my right. I'd suggest you do the same, unless you're a southpaw, and if so, do just the opposite. You can also cradle the bird with an open hand under the back and work on him that way.

STEP 2: Start near the vent, or where the tail feathers disappear into the body, and work *against the grain*—

that is, from tail to head. Dry plucking is no more involved than pinching a clump of feathers between your thumb and forefinger and pulling. Actually, pushing would be a more accurate description. Just slip your thumb in underneath the feathers until it rests against the skin, and push until you've pinched the feathers between your fingers. Tip: Maintaining downward pressure against the skin with your thumb as you s-l-i-d-e it forward toward your index finger will take care of most of the light, downy feathers.

STEP 3: Next you tackle the legs, wings, and neck. Rooster legs are surprisingly easy to pluck, the only problem area being where the feathers meet the scales. Just take your time. There's no one chasing you. I don't pluck the wings completely, although you certainly can, and it does make for a nice traditional presentation. I pluck to the base of the wing and up, say, an inch or so . . . just enough that I won't cut through feathers when I go to remove the wings. As for the neck, I'm a collar man; that is, I'll pluck up to the white ring or collar and call it good. Some folks stop just above the breast; others pluck up to the skull. It's really your choice, but I will say this: Pheasant necks, like chicken necks, make for great soup stock. And did I mention gravy?

STEP 4: Now the bird's nude. Remove the head and that portion of the neck you don't want with a simple cut. Here's where you'll appreciate that knife with a little backbone. Next, with the bird on its right side—left side facing up—grab the wing at the middle joint and pull it up *and* toward the bird's head. You want to expose the pheasant equivalent of your armpit—the wingpit, if you will. Let the weight of the bird help expose that joint, or the pit. Now cut into the pit at about a forty-five-degree angle and perpendicular to a line running from the bird's head to its tail. Pick up just a little bit on the wing and bend it slightly, again toward the head. This should fully expose the joint that connects the wing to the body and, with a little practice, will actually pop the joint out of place. A bit of knife-tip work on the cartilage holding the joint together, and the wing is off. Flip the rooster over, do it again, and the wings are gone.

STEP 5: With the nude, wingless bird on its back, tail to the right, make a cut—again perpendicular to the head-tail line—straight downward and slightly ahead of the vent, completely through the bird's backbone. If you've done it right, you should have two objects in front of you: a good pheasant to your left and a combination of tail and tail feathers to your right. Don't toss the tail just yet; first pluck three to five of the longest tail feathers (see sidebar).

This cut serves three purposes. One, it removes the basically inedible tail (some, I know, will argue that statement) and the tail feathers. Two, the cut opens up the bird so that the innards can be removed. And

three, in removing this entire portion, you've also removed the oil glands, which were located near the base of the tail and had to be removed anyway.

STEP 6: It's time to address any remaining down, pinfeathers—feathers-to-be—and those fine, hairlike follicles that don't look like feathers but really are. For this step, known as singeing, nothing beats a propane torch. With a low to moderate flame, give the bird a once-over. You don't want a flame you can weld with, and you don't want to dink around too long in any one spot. Remember, you're singeing, not cooking here. Once singed, these small feathers can often be easily brushed away. Those that can't are no match for a little water during the final wash and rinse. Tip: If you'll recall, I haven't to this point said anything about cutting the legs off. Why? Because you're going to need something to hold on to while you singe your bird.

STEP 7: Once the singeing is complete, you can remove the legs. With the bird on his back, head away, grab a foot—not leg, but foot—in your left hand, knife at the ready in your right. Pick up as if you were trying to raise the bird off the table. This spreads the knee joint, opening it up and stretching the tendons that connect the upper and lower leg. With your knife, cut perpendicular to the line of the leg bones at the knee, where the upper and lower balls meet. It will take a little practice, but in time, you'll learn exactly where to make that first—and only—necessary cut. Tip: As with the wings, let the weight of the bird help separate the joint.

STEP 8: Gutting, or as the English might say, drawing—either way you phrase it, the end result is the same, and that is entrail removal. There are a couple different methods I use to separate a rooster from his innards. The first involves enlarging, if necessary, the hole at the tail end of the bird and simply scooping the innards out. If you do it this way, make sure you remove the kidneys and lungs. Small, reddish brown organs, the kidneys are located on either side of the backbone just inside the opening you made when you cut the tail section away. The lungs—pink or reddish pink "sponges" slightly larger than your thumb—also

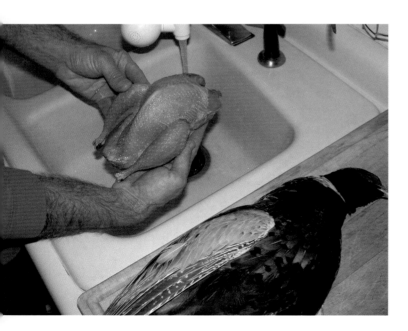

After drawing and singeing, rinse the birds well inside and out before you package them for storage.

Pheasant Feathers

Each year, I save pheasant feathers a couple different ways. Loose feathers from the dry-plucking process—dry feathers, mind you—are put into Ziploc bags and simply stored. Entire skins, on the other hand, are salted lightly or boraxed and hung by the head in the garage out of reach of mice, of which I have many, and black Labs, of which we have three, until they're dry. If for some reason, I do neither, I always, without fail, tug and save the three to five longest tail feathers.

Why do this? One, I'm a firm believer in using every possible part of the game I kill, be it pheasant, mallard, whitetail, or what have you. Second, chances are you know someone who has a use for pheasant feathers. And if you don't, it's easy to find someone.

Ask at a local sporting-goods or fly-fishing shop. Most fly anglers would give their eyeteeth for a steady supply of rooster hackles and other feathers. Craft stores, too, are always looking for something like this. Boy Scouts, Girl Scouts, and church groups are constantly on the lookout for inexpensive, if not free, crafting materials. In the past, I've sent tail feathers to my brother in Texas for projects he's worked on and entire skins to my dear friend Norman Johnson in Washington State, who's used them in the creation of Native American artifacts. Julie, talented artist that she is, has framed tail feathers alongside hunting photographs and has given these prints to friends and family at Christmastime. It's a cliché, yes, but the possibilities really are endless.

---

lie on either side of the spine, but farther up in the chest cavity. You may have to do a little digging and prodding for these, but you'll get them eventually. Oh, and the crop. What you couldn't remove via the tail opening, you should be able to reach through the V-shaped hole formed by the wishbone.

This second method for removing the innards isn't mine, but rather one I borrowed from Delten Rhoades and his folks at Uncle Buck's Lodge in Brewster, Nebraska. Starting with the same tailless, legless, nude, singed bird, flip it over so that it lies breast-down in your left hand. Insert the tip of a set of tin snips—poultry or game shears work well, too—into the tail-end opening, and cut from tail to head on *both* sides of the backbone; then remove the backbone completely. You don't eat the backbone anyway, and if you're worried about waste, you can always toss it into the stockpot. This spine removal aids greatly in the gutting process by allowing you to get everything out, including the hard-to-reach lungs and crop. And don't worry, those of you who like your birds roasted whole: Arranged breast-up in a roaster and on a serving platter, you'd never know that a rooster processed by the whole spine removal method was, indeed, spineless.

STEP 9: Finally, rinse your bird with cool, clean water. Now it's ready for storage.

Scalding

Growing up, I never dry-plucked a rooster pheasant because my father insisted on scalding every bird we were fortunate enough to bring home. "It was good enough for your Dzedo (Slovak grandfather)," he'd tell me, which was a lead-in to his reminder that his father had owned a poultry business for some thirty-five years. At that time, poultry and scalding went together like a hand and glove, so you can see where I'm going with this.

True, scalding is little more than dry-plucking a wet rooster; however, there is an additional piece of equipment on the gear list, as well as an additional step in the scalding process, as compared with the dry method. First, you're going to need either hot tap water or, lacking that, a means of heating water. How hot, you ask? Well, the object of scalding is to use hot water to loosen the feathers, thereby making it possible to pluck the bird without tearing the skin. Simple enough. So how hot is hot? Typically, as hot as the water will come out of your faucet is going to be hot enough to accomplish this task. In my pop's case, his water in the downstairs utility tubs runs from 120 to 130 degrees, and this works just fine. I guess you could heat cool water on the stove and pour it into a larger galvanized bucket. Or in fine frontier style, heat a kettle over a fire in the backyard. However you do it, your first job is to get hot water. If it steams, it's hot enough.

So if water and a bucket large enough to dunk a grown rooster pheasant are the additional pieces of equipment, what's the additional step? That's it— dunking the pheasant in the bucket of hot, steaming water. The trick here is to soak the bird thoroughly without cooking him or changing the ordinary water into the beginnings of pheasant soup. How do you know when he's had enough? You'll know. When he looks soaked, he usually is. Then it's simply a matter of going up to step 2 in the previous section and proceeding as if you were dry-plucking. Yes, you may have to soak him a time or two during the process, but usually once he's wet, he's going to stay that way.

My thoughts on scalding are these: Yes, scalding works as a way of separating the bird from his feathers without—usually—tearing the skin; however, scalding is also messy, what with wet roosters and wet feathers clogging up the sink drain. Too, you're going to need some place where you can do all this soggy work. And finally, there's that, well, that scent. Have you ever smelled a wet chicken? There's a certain funk about a sopping wet rooster pheasant, especially a hot sopping wet rooster pheasant, that's in a category all its own.

Skinning

To me, and I believe to many, skinning pheasants comes with one big plus and one big minus. The plus rests in the fact that skinning is quick. And it's easy, too, should you want to add a secondary positive. On the minus side, however, skinning eliminates one of many folks' favorite parts of the bird—simply, the skin. The skin aids greatly in keeping the bird moist during the cooking process if the bird is cooked whole, which they often are. Ultimately, the decision whether to skin your roosters depends on, one, what you're going to do with them in the kitchen, and two, what emphasis you put on your tabletop presentation. A roasted rooster, skin glowing a golden brown, looks awfully nice when compared with a naked one done the same way. Still, it's up to you. All that said, skinning a pheasant is indeed quick and easy.

STEP 1: With the bird on his back, head away, begin with the knife, blade edge up, and insert just the tip at the point where the breastbone ends above the vent. You want to penetrate the skin only. I use the same Buck Model 224 knife I use for dry plucking.

STEP 2: Slide the blade toward the head, stopping roughly at the V formed by the wishbone. It can help to maintain contact between the spine (backbone) of the knife and the breastbone or keel of the bird. Tip: With practice, you'll be able to make this initial cut without first plucking any of the breast feathers; however, it might be helpful to pluck a line between the vent and the throat area simply as a guide.

STEP 3: Set the knife aside. Now take the first two fingers on each hand and place them inside the cut you've made along the breastbone. Gently work the skin away from the breast while simultaneously pulling in opposite directions. Eventually, the entire breast will be exposed. That's what you want. Peel the skin back on each side past the ribs and down the belly to the vent.

STEP 4: Grab each leg, one at a time, and p-u-s-h while at the same time working the skin from around each thigh and upper leg. Pull the skin, inside out like a glove, down the lower leg to the point where the scales start. Here you can either cut around the leg to loosen the skin or just give it a good yank.

STEP 5: Reread step 5 for the dry-plucking process describing the vertical cut just ahead of or above the vent. You want to duplicate that procedure, with one exception: *Don't cut entirely through the skin on the backside.* It takes a little practice, and you're going to mess up a time or two before you get the knack of cutting through the belly and the backbone (spine) without cutting that thin skin on the lower back . . . but you'll get it.

STEP 6: Flip the partially skinned rooster over, tail to the right. With your left hand—opposite for southpaws—grab the tail portion, while holding the body of the bird in your right. *Carefully* pull in opposite directions. Essentially, you're pulling the entire feathered skin off like a glove. Continue to pull until you reach the wings.

STEP 7: At the wings, there's a little knife work. Expose the joint that connects the wing to the body with a little bending, and use the point of your knife to slice through the skin, flesh, and tendons. Again, with a little practice and some surgical cutting, the wings will pop out of joint. Cut the wings away but leave them attached to the skin. Turn the bird over, and repeat on the opposite side.

STEP 8: Finally, grab both wings and continue pulling the skin upward toward the head and neck.

Once your desired portion of the neck is exposed, make that last cut. On the table lies a wonderfully skinned rooster ready for gutting and a rinse. In your hand is a complete, intact, feathered pheasant skin.

Filleting

If skinning is a drake mallard on the wing, then filleting is a blue-winged teal. And anyone who's ever spent any time in the marsh knows exactly the comparison I speak of. Filleting is, without question, the quickest method of separating the largest portion of edible pheasant flesh from its former owner, a great thing to know how to do if you're pressed for time, have several birds to clean, or are pressed for time *and* have several birds to clean. But filleting also limits what you can do with that edible portion in terms of prep for the table. Too, it's my thinking that if you're filleting—or as it's

also known, breasting—your birds and tossing the legs, thighs, back, and feathers into the trash . . . well, you're wasting a lot of excellent eating, not to mention missing out on a trailer load of trout flies and potential decorations. So there's that. But, yes, filleting is quick and easy:

STEP 1: With the rooster on his back, head away, expose the entire breast. This can be done with a blade, as detailed in the skinning process, or simply by tearing the thin skin of the breast and pulling in opposite directions. Either way works fine.

STEP 2: With the breast exposed, make a cut down to the breastbone on the outside edge of either arm of the V-shaped clavicle, or wishbone. Keep the side of your knife tight against the bone. As you make the cut on the left side of the wishbone, continue down the left side of the keel to the point just above the vent;

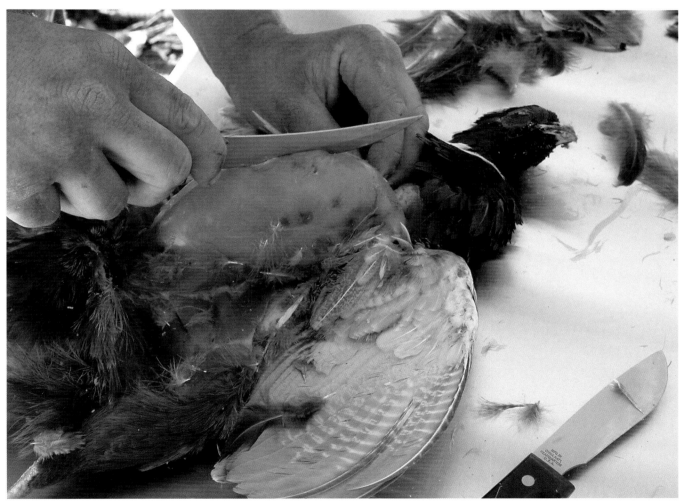

Filleting is quick and easy, and if you also take the legs and thighs for soup, this method leaves very little waste behind.

repeat on the right side. Make sure you keep the side of the blade along the keel and the edge of the blade against the breastbone or breast plate.

STEP 3: Starting on either the left or right side—doesn't matter—and using your thumb, pick up the breast fillet slightly. Slide the edge of your blade down the cut to the breast plate and slice the fillet away from the plate. Work down past the ribs. The tail portion of the fillet will come away first; a little knifework and the thicker portion around the wing joints can be cut free. Repeat on the opposite side.

STEP 4: At this point, some folks are finished; I'm not. I'll skin the legs and thighs by the skinning method described earlier. Detach the whole leg and thigh by pressing the knee away from the body. This pops the thigh out of joint, and with a little knifework, the whole unit can be cut away. Sometimes I'll keep the leg and thigh together; other times I'll separate the two. To me, there's absolutely no reason not to keep the thigh meat. It's darker and can be a little tougher, sure, but stewed or done in a slow cooker, it can be just fine. As for the legs—well, there I'll be a bit more lenient, as the knifelike tendons in a rooster's leg, and there are plenty of 'em, can make both cleaning and eating a truly interesting experience.

STORAGE

If you plan on making pheasant the main attraction at an upcoming meal—and by upcoming, I mean within the next two or three days—then storage consists of little more than a good final rinsing under cold water and a brief respite in a plastic-wrap-covered container in the fridge. As the blood drains from the carcasses, you may find it necessary to drain the container and rerinse the birds, but in terms of storage, it's awfully easy. If, however, pheasant isn't in your immediate future, then you need to package your birds for a longer stay in the deep freeze.

Short-Term Storage

I'm going to define short-term storage as anything up to thirty days in the freezer. The procedure is quite simple. Take your pheasant, and it doesn't matter whether it's whole, breast fillets, legs and thighs, or a combination, and drop it in a quality heavy-duty Ziploc freezer bag. Get it frozen and keep it frozen

until you're ready to use it in the kitchen. Certainly, you can go traditional and cloak your birds first in plastic wrap, then newspaper, and finally, butcher paper; however, though this will indeed do the job, it also seems a bit ambitious for something that's going to be in the freezer for only a month or less.

Long-Term Storage

Here we're talking anything more than thirty days. Now, it's time to get a little more serious.

That old standby, the plastic wrap–newspaper–butcher paper combination, has served me well over the years. I'll typically take it one step further and drop the entire package into a good Ziploc freezer bag. Squeeze out as much air as possible, zip her shut, and your rooster ought to be protected from freezer burn for six months . . . maybe a little longer. Mark the package as to the contents, along with the date it was processed and went into the freezer. Nothing like planning a pheasant dinner and unwrapping the thawed package, only to find two racks of wild Texas hog ribs. Personally, I'd be just fine with that discovery, but some folks might be disappointed. Imagine that?

Waxed milk cartons present another long-term storage option; however, I have to be honest—I've never done this. The method is easy. Take a waxed milk carton and rinse it thoroughly. Drop your whole rooster, headfirst, into the carton. Fillets, bone-in breasts, legs, thighs, it doesn't matter. It can all go into the carton. Fill the carton with just enough water to cover the contents and put it in the freezer. Eventually the water freezes, thus encasing the contents in an airtight shell. After all, it's air or oxygen that causes freezer burn. It all sounds great, and I'm sure it works just fine. The problems I see outweigh the benefits, however. One, you need cartons, which are becoming less common. Two, you need a place in the freezer to place the water-filled cartons upright where they're not going to spill. And three, you then need space enough to store these bulky containers in the freezer once they're frozen. Me? I'll opt for the wrapping or . . .

Vacuum packers. If you're going to package any amount of wild game or fish and expect it to stay as fresh as possible for any length of time in the deep freeze, do yourself a favor and invest in a vacuum packer. No, the units aren't inexpensive, what with

These are goose breast fillets, but my point here is the same—get a vacuum packer. It will pay for itself in excellent, well-kept table fare in no time.

Pheasant halves sizzling away on a Coleman Road Trip Grill. This is one of my favorite bird recipes and also one of the easiest to prepare.

a quality FoodSaver brand unit running anywhere from $125 to $300, depending on the model and features. Then there are the bags, with an eleven-inch-wide by eighteen-foot-long continuous roll—you cut 'em yourself—costing another $20 bill. Still, and the cost certainly considered, you simply cannot do better, if it's proper food storage and protection you want, than a vacuum packer. We use ours, a FoodSaver Professional, not only to encase pheasants and other fowl, but also to package venison, fish fillets, garden vegetables, and bulk foods, to mention just a handful of things. Vacuum packing allows you to keep foods in the freezer for up to a year, maybe even longer, though I know that around here, pheasant doesn't last nearly that long. Bottom line on the vacuum packer? You won't regret the investment.

IN THE KITCHEN

In each of our previous books, I made the announcement that we weren't publishing a cookbook and I wasn't going to spend much time on recipes. And each time, I . . . well, I lied.

Here, though, I'm going to say it again and stick to it. Oh, I have a couple simple recipes that I need to pass along, but for the most part, I'll just say this: If you can do it with chicken, you can do it with pheasant. The only differences are that, one, unlike chickens, pheasants work for a living, and therefore, they don't have the natural fat that fed-daily chickens do, so they require a careful eye and some preplanning in order to keep them moist. And, two, pheasant tastes better.

Phil's Pheasant

"I'm big on roasting plucked pheasants whole," says writing colleague and hunting co-conspirator Phil Bourjaily. And here's his recipe.

Top the bird with a couple strips of bacon or rub a little oil on the skin to keep it moist. Roast for about 45–50 minutes in a 375-degree oven, or until an instant-read thermometer shows 160 degrees when you stick it in the breast. Take the bird out and let it sit for 10 to 15 minutes before carving.

"I usually just slice the meat off the thighs as if it were breast meat," Phil says. "When no one is looking, I go back into the kitchen and gnaw on the carcass."

The man's honest. . . .

Rooster à la Mick

My pop, Mick, does this with rabbit and squirrel, and it's absolutely wonderful. Several years ago, I substituted pheasant for the furry four-legged critters, and I have been doing it this way ever since. It's simple, though maybe a bit time-consuming; still, it's incredibly good and feeds a ton of people.

You can work with either pheasant breasts and thighs or whole birds that have been cut in half. I like the whole halves, as the bone-in element seems to help keep the birds moist throughout the cooking process. That in mind, we'll work here with whole halves.

Wash four pheasant halves—two whole birds split lengthwise—and pat dry. Dip each half in an egg-milk mixture, let drain somewhat, and then toss in a Ziploc bag containing flour, salt, pepper, garlic powder, Old Bay seasoning, and—for me—a little cayenne. Brown the dusted birds on both sides in a hot skillet with a little olive oil. Set them aside on a paper plate covered in paper towel to drain a bit.

Next, you're going to need the following. This is improvisation at its finest, however, so your list may, and probably will, differ:

> 1 can cream of mushroom soup
> Orange juice—or cranberry, apple, or grapefruit juice
> 2 cans of diced tomatoes (I like the kind with onions, peppers, and chilis)
> Sweet (Vidalia or Walla Walla) onion, sliced
> 2 cans mushrooms, stems and pieces
> Half-inch slices of hot Italian sausage, pepperoni, deer sausage—some kind of sausage
> Whole jalapeño peppers, sliced lengthwise and seeded
> 1 orange, cut in half
> Watkins garlic oil

Get a heavy roaster. (We use an old four-quart Wagner Ware round iron roaster.) Mix the cream of mushroom soup with the juice of your choice, using one and a half times the amount of liquid called for. Pour a little bit of the soup-juice mixture in the bottom of the roaster, just enough to cover the bottom.

Next, spoon in some of the tomatoes, again, just enough to cover the bottom. Make a layer of onions, toss in a handful of mushrooms, and add a few slices of sausage. Lay on a pheasant half or two, depending on the size of your roaster, and a slice of jalapeño. Pour a little more of your soup-juice mixture over top of the bird, then add some more onions, mushrooms, sausage. You see, it's a layering thing.

Continue building your layers until all the ingredients are in the pot. Pour any remaining soup-juice mixture over the layers, and add a couple more slices of jalapeño. Squeeze the juice from one orange over the whole thing and drop the halves, peel and all, into the roaster along an edge. Drizzle a little garlic oil over the top of everything.

Roast in the oven at 350 degrees for an hour and a half. Serve over steamed white rice.

Smoking, Please . . .

Some folks, I'm sure, will disagree, but the only thing better in my opinion than smoked pheasant is smoked sturgeon; however, because this is a *pheasant-hunting* book, and I've seldom run into roosters in the Columbia River Gorge below Bonneville Dam, we'll stick with the ringnecks.

It's easy to be intimidated by the game-smoking process, but smoking wild game, be it birds, fish, venison, or whatever, is actually quite simple. Sure, it takes a little experimentation, and your first attempts might not be the most wonderful culinary experiences you've ever enjoyed; still, smoking wild meats, like the art that is cooking, is a thing of trial and error. Hell, how do you figure yogurt was invented? Or cottage cheese? I'm sure no one meant to make cottage cheese. But I digress. . . .

If you don't already own one, a smoker is going to be your first issue. Some enterprising folks build their own, salvaging an old refrigerator or freezer and resurrecting it—and in some cases, quite well I must say—as a smoker. Not a do-it-yourselfer? That's not a problem, as there are plenty of commercially produced smokers on the market today. My personal unit is a Big Chief top-loader from Luhr-Jensen—as simple and yet as effective a machine as I've ever used. And inexpensive, too, with even the most modern versions costing less than $100. Certainly, you can spend more money. If you happen to have $250 burning a hole in your britches, the self-loading electric

From grill to table takes but a few minutes.

Bradley Smoker is a fantastic way to smoke any number of different meats and fish. So, too, is Cabela's stack rack (vertical) propane-driven unit. Whatever kind you use—big, small, electric, propane, home-made—the end result can be a wonderful wild treat made for any dining occasion. And did I mention that smoked pheasant, like smoked sturgeon, goes great with beer?

The smoking process consists of three steps—brining, smoking, and cooking. First, the bird—and I use skin-on birds carefully plucked whole—is brined, soaked in a salt-based solution for six to twelve hours. Everyone has his or her own favorite brining recipe. Here's mine for pheasants:

$^1/_2$ cup noniodized or pickling salt
$^1/_2$ cup white sugar
1 quart cold water (I like distilled water—
      fewer impurities)

To this, I'll add in amounts to suit my taste:

Garlic oil
Black pepper
Cayenne pepper
Onion powder
Worcestershire sauce
Tabasco
Orange juice
White wine

Your list of ingredients and your taste will likely be different. Experimentation is not only key, but fun.

Once all the ingredients are mixed and dissolved, pour the brine into a tall, wide-mouthed glass—never use a wood or aluminum—container; something like a large pickle jar works very well. Drop in one or two birds, cover the jar with plastic wrap secured with a rubber band around the neck, and leave it in the fridge overnight. I brine my fish and game a bit longer than most, sometimes twenty-four hours or more depending on how much flavor I want and what I'm working with.

Once the birds have brined to your liking, towel them off and put them into the smoker. I've made heavy wire hooks with which I hang my roosters from the top rack in the Big Chief—all the other racks having been removed. You can use the racks should you wish; however, make sure to flip the birds at least once during the smoking process. How long should you

*Slow-cooked bone-in pheasant breasts with some mushrooms and some potatoes
and a little cream of mushroom soup . . . wow!*

smoke? Two hours for a light smoke, four to six for a heavier flavor. Use anywhere from two to three or slightly more pans of chips, or the equivalent in briquettes should your unit be a Bradley or similar machine. Regardless of how long the birds remain in the smoker, you want to remember that this part of the process is flavoring *not* cooking.

With the birds sufficiently flavored, simply place them on a rack in a roaster to which you've added a little bit of water, white wine, and garlic oil. Cover with heavy-duty aluminum foil, and roast in a 350-degree oven for an hour or so. It tastes fancy, but it isn't.

Simply Slow Cooking

I realize I said that this wasn't going to be a cookbook; still, there are at least a couple pheasant recipes that I think everyone should try once in his or her lifetime.

If you do, there's a damn good chance you'll try it again. And again.

This is a very simple recipe, though on the surface it appears quite complicated. It's great for company or, as we've done in the past, manufactured in an eighteen- or twenty-two-quart roaster oven and used as a popular main dish at a potluck, reception, picnic, or anywhere there's a lot of folks to feed—that is, if you're not hesitant about sharing your roosters. Anyway, here are the ingredients for a recipe for four:

Milk
1 egg beaten
Flour
Salt
Garlic powder
Pepper
Olive oil
White wine

There's no such thing as having no appetite when wild pheasant is on the menu—at least not for me.

1 can cream of mushroom soup
1 can cream of chicken soup
1 small can sliced mushrooms
3 cups orange juice
Half a sweet onion, sliced
Fresh asparagus

Start with two whole birds cut into three pieces: leg and thigh, and bone-in breast complete. You can also use the back, if you wish; I don't, but instead use the backs in my crawdad traps—your call. Dip the pieces in a little bit of milk to which you've added a beaten egg, and then shake each piece in a Ziploc bag containing flour, salt, garlic powder, and pepper. Put a little olive oil in a heavy skillet or slow cooker—I use an old Griswold no. 8 deep-sided chicken fryer—and brown the meat on both sides. Remove and set aside. Deglaze the skillet with a bit of white wine, but *don't* throw away the brown crumbly nuggets that result. Those are excellent.

In a mixing bowl, combine the cream of mushroom and cream of chicken soups. Toss in the sliced mushrooms, followed by the orange juice, and whisk together. Pour about a quarter to a half inch into the bottom of the skillet or slow-cooker, then a layer of pheasant. Cover this with onion slices. Add more liquid, then more pheasant until all the bird is gone. Put a handful of fresh asparagus spears on top and pour in a little more liquid. Cover with a lid and turn the heat down to low. Cooking time is about two hours, or as long as you can resist the aroma without getting into the pot. Serve over rice or wide egg noodles.

If you're so inclined, you can spice up the recipe by adding a couple hunks of hot Italian sausage or, as I've been known to do, a piece or two of spicy deer pepperoni, to the middle layers. Pineapple chunks or mandarin oranges on top about halfway through the process are also good. The possibilities are almost endless.

CHAPTER 8

The Pheasant's Future

U P TO THIS POINT—AS MAY BE PAINFULLY obvious from time to time—I've tried not to project a negative, "no pheasants ere" attitude in my dialogue. And I have to admit that at times, it's been a tough task, this staying optimistic about a wild population that in my youth I barely knew and that today I see, well, slowly fading away in many parts of the country. No water in Nebraska and Kansas. A switch from grains to grapes in eastern Washington and California. Fields tilled and farmed within an inch of the barbed wire in Iowa. The perilous day-to-day existence of the Conservation Reserve Program (CRP), the governmental program that pays farmers to set ground aside and produce not corn or soybeans, but vital nesting and wintering habitat . . . and pheasants.

But what's it all mean? First, let me preface this brief explanation with the statement that I am not a schooled wildlife manager or biologist. I don't pretend to know all of the intricacies involved with every microphyte community in existence; however, and while I will admit that it's most elemental, what I do know is this. If given a place to live, pheasants will do just that: live. Food, water, and shelter, where shelter in terms of the ringneck can be defined as grassy nesting cover and thicker, protective wintering and loafing cover. To the best of my knowledge, it's really no more complicated than that.

What is the future of pheasant hunting in the United States? Only time, and the conservation efforts of many, will tell. SOUTH DAKOTA TOURISM

PHEASANTS FOREVER

That's where Pheasants Forever (PF) comes in. Founded in 1982, PF's goal, as is put forth in its mission statement, is "to conserve and to enhance pheasant and other wildlife populations through habitat restoration, improvements in land, water, and wildlife management policies, and public awareness and education." In a nutshell, this can be translated to read as giving pheasants a place to live and letting folks know (1) that pheasants need these places, (2) what kind of places these birds actually need, and perhaps most important, (3) how people can get involved and what they can realistically do, as the organization's goal states, to conserve and enhance pheasant and other wild populations simply by contributing to the world around them.

Joe Duggan, PF vice president of development and public affairs, has this to say about the Minnesota-based organization: "Pheasants Forever's focus is on conserving, enhancing, and increasing the quantity and quality of wildlife habitat. And in doing projects that we typically do—native grass restoration for nesting cover, wetland restoration to enhance winter cover, planting farmstead shelterbelts—we're doing a couple things. In addition to specifically addressing the needs of pheasants—well, for instance, some of the most endangered and threatened wildlife species are the neotropical migrants that inhabit the prairie regions of North America. They're benefiting tremendously from our work. We've done stream and riparian restoration projects in the West that have had tremendous benefits to native trout and native trout streams. The benefits to wildlife are across the board. When you stick vegetative cover on the ground where it wasn't before, you're going to provide a place for wildlife to live. And when we improve the quality and quantity of that vegetative cover we call wildlife habitat, you're making spaces for other wildlife and critters to live."

But the question remains, is it working?

It's all about the habitat. Give them a place to live and they'll do just fine. SOUTH DAKOTA TOURISM

Pheasants Forever members such as this gentleman enjoying South Dakota's hospitality wear their affiliation proudly—as they should.

Habitat is important year-round, yet it becomes even more crucial during the winter and the nesting period in late spring and early summer.

Good pheasant habitat creates food sources and living quarters for an almost endless array
of game and nongame species, including these Merriam's turkeys.

"You do see benefits," says Duggan. "Sometimes they're immediate, and sometimes they take time. But when you install the habitat practices that we do—the nesting cover, the wetland restoration, the shelterbelts, the buffer strips—within a year or two, there is a physical difference in the landscape that you can actually see. And wildlife will move into these new areas very rapidly, and you'll start seeing pheasants and other wildlife occupying that space.

"Here's one of my favorite quotes on that very subject. A good friend of mine hunts South Dakota every year. He and a farmer were actually talking about the Conservation Reserve Program and what happens if the CRP program goes away. Greg says that the farmer told him, 'Until we enrolled this ground in CRP, we didn't have pheasants around here. Not like we have today.' And Greg asked him, 'What happens if you lose that CRP?' The farmer said, 'See that field across the road?' pointing to a field that was all plowed and under

intensive agriculture. 'That's what it'll all get back to. Away will go the habitat, and away will go the pheasants. You know something?' the farmer continued. 'That stuff they call habitat? That stuff really works.'"

According to documentation that Duggan provided my wife and me during a three-day outing with him in South Dakota in the fall of 2002, PF has, since its inception in 1982, developed more than two million acres of what it refers to as "pheasant and other wildlife habitat." This, along with the organization's more than thirty thousand successfully completed projects and programs, has been accomplished, Duggan proudly reminded us, by some ninety-two thousand members, all of whom are volunteering their time, effort, and, yes, money. What's more, PF currently has more than four thousand teachers and other education professionals spreading the conservation word via the organization's Leopold Education Project.

Awe-inspiring is the view above the Missouri River in central South Dakota, one of the last bastions for healthy populations of wild ringnecks in the United States.

"The Leopold Education Project is a multidisciplinary curriculum that is based on the writings of Aldo Leopold and *The Sand County Almanac*," Duggan explains. "The objective is, through critical thinking skills and teaching those skills, all learned through *The Sand County Almanac*, to provide the next generation with an understanding of the land and how it connects to us all. And by giving them critical thinking skills, they'll come to know the difference between a fact and a value. They in turn will make assessments about how humankind is tied to the land and how that knowledge is important. The goal of the project is to try to instill that land ethic in our nation's youth. We're educating thousands of educators each year on the Leopold Education Project and its curriculum."

In the same way that National Wild Turkey Federation efforts benefit whitetails and Ducks Unlimited projects provide for sandhill cranes and white-fronted geese, so too are PF undertakings helping secure the

The best of both worlds—a member of Pheasants Forever and a youth mentor program participant. We desperately need more gentlemen like this.

Young men such as Gordon Bourjaily, here with Ike, represent the future of hunting in this country. Are you doing your part to see that they have the opportunity? PHIL BOURJAILY

future not only for the ringneck, but also for any of a hundred thousand wild, wonderful, and oh-so-irreplaceable things, including our own hunting heritage as well as that of our children and their children. For more on Pheasants Forever, take a few minutes and visit the organizations's website at www.pheasantsforever.org. Or better yet, call PF at 877-773-2070. I'm not much on "pawl-a-tick'n," but the pheasant hunters you'll reach at this number will certainly be glad you picked up the telephone.

ROOSTERS AND YOUTH: PASSING THE TORCH

Over the past twenty years, whitetails—big bucks and huge antlers—have stolen the hunting limelight. That's unfortunate, I think, for in doing so, these animals have

Left: Hunter education is a wonderful and often mandatory first step; however, learning shouldn't end there.
Below: Does your state offer youth pheasant-hunting opportunities? If so, are you out there mentoring? If not, why not? Youth hunting opportunities are everyone's concern.

Above: A young, fresh face and a field-worn side-by-side shotgun—tell me, does it really get much better?
Left: Iowa's Marshall Dusheck is the next generation of all-around hunters, and it's up to us to see that they're coached with the knowledge they need to be successful.

overshadowed one of the finest outdoor traditions ever enjoyed in this country—small-game hunting. Today the pheasant hunters are few in comparison to the whitetailists, and smaller still is the population of those who thrill at the sounds of beagle on track or the telltale shudder of a shagbark hickory branch high in the September canopy. But . . . I'll try not to wax nostalgic for days—and small-game hunters—gone by. Instead, let's think constructively. A glass-half-full kind of proposition. And the topic at hand? How to bring more young hunters into the fold, one, and two, the methods by which to see to it that these young guns are exposed to the joys of small-game hunting— notably, pheasant hunting.

Hunter Education
It's my belief that if hunter education is going to be mandatory for all first-time hunters, then all hunters should at one time or another either become certified volunteer instructors or at the very least involve them-

selves in some way. You don't have to teach a course from start to finish. Perhaps you handle only the shotgunning portion. Or the upland-bird-hunting section. Or the portion on safety. Regardless of your role, I believe you should play one—a role, that is. The bottom line is this: Get involved. This isn't "the other guy's" responsibility; it's your responsibility. And mine.

Youth Hunting Opportunities
If your state offers a youth pheasant season, take advantage of it. Don't have a young hunter of your own? Then make yourself available as a licensed adult supervisor by joining in or initiating an organized youth pheasant hunt through your local Izaak Walton League, gun club, Boy or Girl Scout troop, or sporting-goods store. Pheasants Forever on the state level can be very helpful in uniting young hunters with future mentors. As I mentioned previously, the bottom line is to get involved.

Whether in Ohio, South Dakota, Montana, or eastern Washington, the tradition that is pheasant hunting should not be allowed to fade from the whole of the outdoors. SOUTH DAKOTA TOURISM

Long Seasons Equal Lots of Opportunity

Think about it. Deer season—gun season, that is—lasts what, five days? Maybe two weeks, depending on where you are. There are exceptions, most notably in some of the southern states, where deer gun seasons may be months long; however, in many cases, the opportunities for a young person to hunt deer when the proverbial gettin' is good are relatively short-lived. Now let's look at pheasant season. Here in Iowa, for instance, pheasant hunters enjoy a season that stretches some nine weeks. Go to South Dakota, and it's eleven weeks.

But let's take this discussion a step further and look at licensed shooting preserves. Most open on September 1 and close April 1. That's seven months, or twenty-eight weeks if my math skills prove correct—of pheasant-hunting bliss. Combine this with the fact that most shooting preserves offer discounted youth rates, especially toward the end of their business year, and ah, yes . . . the light's starting to flicker.

It's like fishing, folks. If you want to get a kid to get hooked on fishing, you don't take him chasing muskies.

Hell, if you did, he might go two, three years before he ever gets a strike, if then. No, you take him to the local farm pond and have him catch one bluegill after another after another after another. Likewise, if you want your young charge to first get interested in upland hunting and then stay interested, you want to take him someplace where he's going to have opportunities to shoot at winged game. Purists, take heart. Wild pheasants will come, as will the frustrations associated with them. First, however, allow the youngster the experience a well-run preserve can afford—it *can* make a difference.

Why Not Small-Game Hunting?

Let me be perfectly blunt: I don't know what all the hubbub is about those big, old white-tailed deer. And I certainly don't understand why they commandeer all the attention these days. Ego maybe? Money? Status? Perhaps it's a little of all three. Now don't get me wrong; I'm not anti-whitetail. In fact, I love them just fine all wrapped up in butcher paper and living right alongside the wild turkey breasts and whole plucked roosters in the basement freezer.

No, my biggest complaint about today's whitetail mania stems from what the pursuit of the next world-record rack has done to small-game hunting in the United States; that is, it's practically done away with it. So I'm going to take this opportunity now, and primarily because it's my book, dammit, and ask you, my reader, for a favor: Please, whatever you do, don't forget small-game hunting. Try not to get caught up in the glamour and glitz that is the white-tailed deer. Instead, or at the very least in addition, take your son or daughter or nephew or the kid next door pheasant hunting. Or squirrel hunting. Or rabbit hunting.

Roosters are quite capable of teaching your nimrod the fundamentals of gun safety, sportsmanship, marksmanship, ethical hunting behavior, self-discipline, restraint, public relations, and so on, every bit as well as, if not better than the white-tailed deer—if, that is, you let them. Trust me on this one . . . you'll be glad you did.

Random Thoughts at Closing Time

It's been twenty-five years, I guess, but today, right here and now, we could get in my grandpa's old Chevy pickup and I could take you to the farm in northeastern Ohio where I killed my first wild rooster pheasant. I'm not sure what's there now; haven't been back in . . . well, damn near twenty-five years. Hell, we might be standing in the middle of a Wal-Mart parking lot, for all I know, but I could take you there—maybe, if the east woods still exist, within a few yards of where it happened. My dad was there—he'll remember, perhaps better than me.

When we're done there, we'll drive a couple hours south and west to a farm not far from the outskirts of the state capital. It was the first and only two-bird limit of Ohio roosters I ever killed—young birds, not fully colored, but that thought never entered my mind until later. Later in life, that is. Jim Wentz was there; in fact, I was his guest that morning. For years, Wentz commanded Ohio's Hunter Education Section—Outdoor Skills Unit, pardon me—and as such was instrumental in introducing thousands of young people to the wonders of the field. Today Jim owns Silvertip Productions, a "motion picture production and Internet development" company specializing in topics such as fishing, wildlife, and outdoor recreation, and he remains very active in hunter education and fish-and-game agencies across the country and around the globe. His was, and continues to be, a life dedicated to opening the doors to the Great Outdoors. Everyone should have a Jim Wentz; I'm glad I had mine.

In northcentral Oregon's Tygh Valley, the man's name was Bruce Meredith. In Nebraska, it was Delten Rhoades. It was Richard Kieffer in South Dakota, Phil Bourjaily in Iowa, Neal Verity in Ohio . . . and the list goes on and on. I mention these men for a reason. You see, pheasant hunting is about the people and places. Oh, it's about that grand upland bird, the ringneck, certainly, for his role in the Grand Scheme of Things is, indeed, most vital. But truthfully? It's about the people. It's about the characters, the curmudgeons. The guides, the outfitters. The truth seekers and the storytellers. They don't enrich the experience, as so many an outdoor writer might say. No, they *are* the experience. Without them, there is no truth. There is no story. Without them, the act would be shooting, not hunting.

You ready? Well, here's as philosophical and as eloquent as I'm going to get. Roosters, for me, have been a conduit to something spiritually better. They've taken me to places and handed me to people that I never would have seen or met. In short, my world has been vastly improved by the ringneck's presence. And that's it; that's all there is to it. Melodramatic? I don't think so, because I believe that if you ask any pheasant hunter how his world would be changed if tomorrow all the birds were to disappear, he'd answer, and rather quickly: What world?

That's what I'm talking about.

*Hunters mustn't let the sun set on the tradition that is upland bird hunting,
but this salvation will require effort from all of us.*

Manufacturers, Outfitters, and Agencies

MANUFACTURERS

These are the folks who make the *stuff* that makes pheasant hunting more convenient and perhaps more successful. I use this stuff. This isn't a wish list or an advertisement. These companies make good gear, plain and simple, and they are all worth looking into.

Arborwear
P.O. Box 341
Chagrin Falls, OH 44022
1-888-578-TREE
www.arborwear.com

Avery Outdoors
P.O. Box 820176
Memphis, TN 38112
901-324-1500
www.averyoutdoors.com

Bass Pro Shops
2500 E. Kearney
Springfield, MO 65898
www.basspro.com

Beretta USA
17601 Beretta Drive
Accokeek, MD 20607
www.berettausa.com

Birchwood Casey
7900 Fuller Road
Eden Prairie, MN 55344
www.birchwoodcasy.com

Browning
One Browning Place
Morgan, UT 84050
www.browning.com

Bushnell Sports Optics
9200 Cody
Overland Park, KS 66214
www.bushnell.com

Cabela's
One Cabela's Drive
Sidney, NE 69160
www.cabelas.com

Columbia Sportswear Company
6600 N. Baltimore
Portland, OR 97283
www.columbia.com

DeLorme Mapping
Two Delorme Drive
Yarmouth, ME 04096
www.delorme.com

Federal Cartridge Company (Blount, Inc.)
900 Ehlen Drive
Anoka, MN 55303
www.federalcartridge.com

C. C. Filson
P.O. Box 34020
Seattle, WA 98124
www.filson.com

Gerber Legendary Blades
14200 SW 72nd Avenue
Portland, OR 97223
www.gerberblades.com

Griffin & Howe
33 Claremont Road
Bernardsville, NJ 07924
www.griffinhowe.com

Heatmax, Inc.
505 Hill Road
Dalton, GA 30722
www.heatmax.com

Innotek, Inc.
1000 Fuller Drive
Garrett, IN 46738
www.innotek.net

Kent Cartridge America, Inc.
P.O. Box 849
Kearneysville, WV 25430
www.kentgamebore.com

Kershaw Knives
25300 SW Parkway Avenue
Wilsonville, OR 97070
503-682-1966
www.kershawknives.com

Leatherman Tool Group, Inc.
P.O. Box 20595
Portland, OR 97294
www.leatherman.com

O. F. Mossberg & Sons
7 Grasso Avenue
North Haven, CT 06473
www.mossberg.com

Mossy Oak Clothing—Haas Outdoors
P.O. Box 757
West Point, MS 39773
www.mossyoak.com

Nikon Sport Optics
1300 Walt Whitman Road
Melville, NY 11747
www.nikonusa.com

Ralston Purina
Checkerboard Square
St. Louis, MO 63164
1-800-7-PURINA
www.purina.com/home.aspx

Realtree Outdoor Products, Inc.
P.O. Box 9638
Columbus, GA 31908
www.realtree.com

Remington Arms Company
870 Remington Drive
Madison, NC 27025
www.remington.com

Rocky Shoes & Boots, Inc.
39 Canal Street
Nelsonville, OH 45764
www.rockyboots.com

Tender Corporation
P.O. Box 290
Littleton Industrial Park
Littleton, NH 03561
www.tendercorp.com

Tri-Tronics, Inc.
1705 South Research Loop
Tucson, AZ 85710
www.tritronics.com

Winchester Ammunition
427 N. Shamrock Street
East Alton, IL 49685
www.winchester.com

Winchester Firearms
344 Winchester Avenue
New Haven, CT 06511
1-800-333-3504
www.winchesterguns.com

OUTFITTERS

I have personally worked with the outfitters listed below and can with confidence vouch for their operations. For additional outfitters and shooting preserves, refer to *Black's Wing & Clay, Waterfowl* or visit www.wingshootingusa.org.

Arrowhead Hunt Club
Dan Mullin
3529 170th Street
Goose Lake, IA 52750
563-577-2267

Big Bend Ranch
Alex Falk
1301 N. Fourth Street
Aberdeen, SD 57401
605-229-3035

Bruns Farms Hunts
Bill Bruns
10607 397th Avenue
Hecla, SD 57446
605-885-6324
www.angelfire.com/sd2/brunsfarms

Dakota Expeditions
Clint Smith
19750 356th Avenue
Miller, SD 57362
605-853-2545

Funkrest, Inc.
Don & Bonnie Funk
R.R. 3, Box 167
Madison, SD 57042
605-256-3636

Horsefeathers Lodge
Bob Tinker
3031 Sussex Place
Pierre, SD 57501
605-224-2022

K & M Hunting
Michael and Kathye Miller
38960 256th Street
Plankinton, SD 57368
605-942-7516

Kieffer Pheasant Hunting
Richard & Diana Kieffer
37361 257th Street
White Lake, SD 57383
605-249-2464
www.kiefferhunting.com

Mallardith NW Adventures
Bruce Meredith
81025 E. Wapinitia Road
Maupin, OR 97037
541-980-1922
www.mallardith.com

Rock Creek Lodge
Dennis & Rod Brakke
24935 416th Avenue
Fulton, SD 57340
605-996-9301
www.southdakotapheasants.com

Running Spring Farm
Bill Cork
P.O. Box 105
Everton, MO 65646
417-535-4190
www.runningspringfarm.com

Sandhills Adventures
Delten & Tracy Rhoades
P.O. Box 152
Brewster, NE 68821
www.sandhills-adventures.com

Steve Fahey
Cherokee Charters
P.O. Box 1142
Pierre, SD 57501
605-280-1902
www.cherokeecharter.com

Thunderstik Lodge
R.R. 1, Box 10T
Chamberlain, SD 57325
800-888-1601

Tumbleweed Lodge
Michael Bollweg
20239 321st Avenue
Harrold, SD 57536
800-288-5774

Warne Ranches
Cody Warne
29774 192nd Street
Onida, SD 57564
605-264-5325

AGENCIES

In addition to the good people at the state fish and
game agencies, you can also get information from the
state departments of travel and tourism. From lodging
to where to find the best in good, old-fashioned home
cooking while you're on the road, these folks will be
able to advise you or know someone who can.

Alabama Bureau of Tourism & Travel
401 Adams
Montgomery, AL 36103
800-ALABAMA
www.state.al.us

Alaska Division of Tourism
P.O. Box 110801
Juneau, AK 99811
800-76-ALASKA
www.travelalaska.com

Arizona Office of Tourism
2702 N. Third Street
Phoenix, AZ 85004
800-842-8257
www.arizonaguide.com

Arkansas Department of Parks & Tourism
One Capital Mall
Little Rock, AR 72201
800-NATURAL
www.1800natural.com

California Division of Tourism
801 K Street
Sacramento, CA 95814
800-TO-CALIF
www.gocalif.ca.gov

Colorado Travel & Tourism Authority
1127 Pennsylvania Avenue
Denver, CO 80203
800-COLORADO
www.colorado.com

Connecticut Office of Tourism
505 Hudson Street
Hartford, CT 06106
800-CT-BOUND
www.state.ct.us/tourism

Delaware Tourism Office
99 Kings Highway
Dover, DE 19901
800-441-8846
www.state.de.us/tourism/intro.htm

VISIT FLORIDA
3550 Biscayne Boulevard
Miami, FL 33137
904-487-1462
www.flausa.com

Georgia Department of Industry, Trade, and Tourism
285 Peachtree Center Avenue NE
Atlanta, GA 30303
800-VISIT-GA
www.georgia.org/itt/tourism/

Idaho Division of Tourism Development
700 W. State Street
Boise, ID 83720
800-635-7820
www.visitid.org

Illinois Bureau of Tourism
100 W. Randolph
Chicago, IL 60601
800-2-CONNECT
www.enjoyillinois.com

Indiana Tourism Division
One North Capitol
Indianapolis. IN 46204
800-289-6646
www.ai.org/tourism

Iowa Division of Tourism
200 E. Grand Avenue
Des Moines, IA 50309
800-345-IOWA
www.traveliowa.com

Kansas Travel & Tourism
700 S.W. Harrison Street
Topeka, KS 66603
800-2KANSAS
www.state.ks.us/

Kentucky Department of Travel
500 Mero Street
Frankfort, KY 40601
800/225-TRIP
www.state.ky.us/tour/tour.htm

Louisiana Office of Tourism
1051 N. Third Street
Baton Rouge, LA 70804
800-334-8626
www.louisianatravel.com

Maine Office of Tourism
33 Stone Street
Augusta, ME 04333
800-533-9595
www.visitmaine.com

Maryland Office of Tourism Development
217 E. Redwood Street
Baltimore, MD 45454
800-543-1036
www.mdisfun.org

Massachusetts Office of Travel & Tourism
100 Cambridge Street
Boston, MA 02202
800-447-MASS
www.mass-vacation.com

Travel Michigan
P.O. Box 30226
Lansing, MI, 48909
888-78-GREAT
www.michigan.org

Minnesota Office of Tourism
121 E. Seventh Place
St. Paul, MN 55101
800-657-3700
www.exploreminnesota.com

Mississippi Division of Tourism Development
550 High Street
Jackson, MS 39205
800-WARMEST
www.visitmississippi.org

Missouri Division of Tourism
P.O. Box 1055
Jefferson City, MO 65102
800-877-1234
www.ecodev.state.mo.us/tourism/

Travel Montana
1424 Ninth Avenue
Helena, MT 59620
800-VISIT-MT
www.travel.mt.gov

Nebraska Division of Travel & Tourism
P.O. Box 98907
Lincoln, NE 68509
800-228-4307
www.visitnebraska.org

Nevada Commission on Tourism
401 N. Carson Street
Carson City, NE 89701
800-NEVADA-8
www.travelnevada.com/

New Hampshire Office of Travel & Tourism Dept.
P.O. Box 1856
Concord, NH 03302
800-FUN-IN-NH
www.visitnh.gov

New Jersey Tourism Division
20 W. State Street
Trenton, NJ 08625
800-JERSEY-7
www.state,nj.us/travel

New Mexico Department of Tourism
491 Old Santa Fe Trail
Santa Fe, NM 87503
800-545-2040
www.newmexico.org

New York State Division of Tourism
P.O. Box 2603
Albany, NY 12220
800-CALL-NYS
www.iloveny.state.ny.us

North Carolina Division of Tourism
301 N. Wilmington Street
Raleigh, NC 27601
800-VISIT-NC
www.visitnc.com

North Dakota Tourism Department
604 E. Boulevard Avenue
Bismarck, ND 58505
800-HELLO-ND
www.glness.com/tourism/

Ohio Division of Travel and Tourism
P.O. Box 1001
Columbus, OH 43216
800-BUCKEYE
www.ohiotourism.com

Oklahoma Tourism & Recreation Department
15 N. Robinson
Oklahoma City, OK 73102
800-652-6552
www.otrd.state.ok.us

Oregon Tourism Commission
775 Summer Street NE
Salem, OR 97310
800-547-7842
www.traveloregon.com

Pennsylvania Center for Travel, Tourism, & Film
404 Forum Building
Harrisburg, PA 17120
800-VISIT-PA
www.state.pa.us/visit

Rhode Island Economic Development Corp.
One W. Exchange Street
Providence, RI 02903
800-556-2484
www.visitrhodeisland.com

South Carolina Dept. of Parks, Recreation, & Tourism
1205 Pendleton Street
Columbia, SC 29201
800-346-3634
www.sccsi.com/sc/

South Dakota Department of Tourist Development
711 E. Wells Avenue
Pierre, SD 57501
800-SDAKOTA
www.state.sd.us/tourism

Tennessee Department of Tourist Development
320 Sixth Avenue N
Nashville, TN 37202
800-836-6200
www.state.tn.us/tourdev/

Texas Tourism Division
P.O. Box 12728
Austin, TX 78711
800-88-88-TEX
www.traveltex.com

UTAH!
Council Hall
Salt Lake City, UT 84114
800-200-1160
www.utah.com

Vermont Department of Tourism and Marketing
6 Baldwin Street, Drawer 33
Montpelier, VT 05633
800-VERMONT
www.travel-vermont.com

Virginia Tourism Corporation
901 E. Byrd Street
Richmond, VA 23219
800-VISIT-VA
www.viginia.org

Washington State Tourism
P.O. Box 42500
Olympia, WA 98504
800-544-1800
www.tourism.wa.gov

West Virginia Division of Tourism
2101 Washington Street E
Charleston, WV 25305
800-225-5982
www.state.wv.us/tourism

Wisconsin Department of Tourism
201 W. Washington Avenue
Madison, WI 53707
800-432-TRIP
www.tourism.state.wi.us

Wyoming Business Council Tourism Office
I-25 & College Drive
Cheyenne, WY 82002
800-225-5996
www.state.wy.us/state/tourism